Samuel Taylor Coleridge

the rime of the ancient mariner

Hunt Emerson

colour by Carol Bennett

Dedicated to my Dad

The Rime of the Ancient Mariner
by Samuel Taylor Coleridge and Hunt Emerson
Copyright © 1989 Knockabout Comics
Published by Knockabout Comics,
10 Acklam Road, London W10 5QZ
Colour Carol Bennett. Design Rian Hughes
Technical adviser Jonathan Tatlow
Thanks to Ferid, and to Hermione, Peter and the girls
This edition not for sale in the USA or Canada
ISBN 0 86166 065 X
Printed in Denmark by Norhaven A/S
10 9 8 7 6 5 4 3 2 1

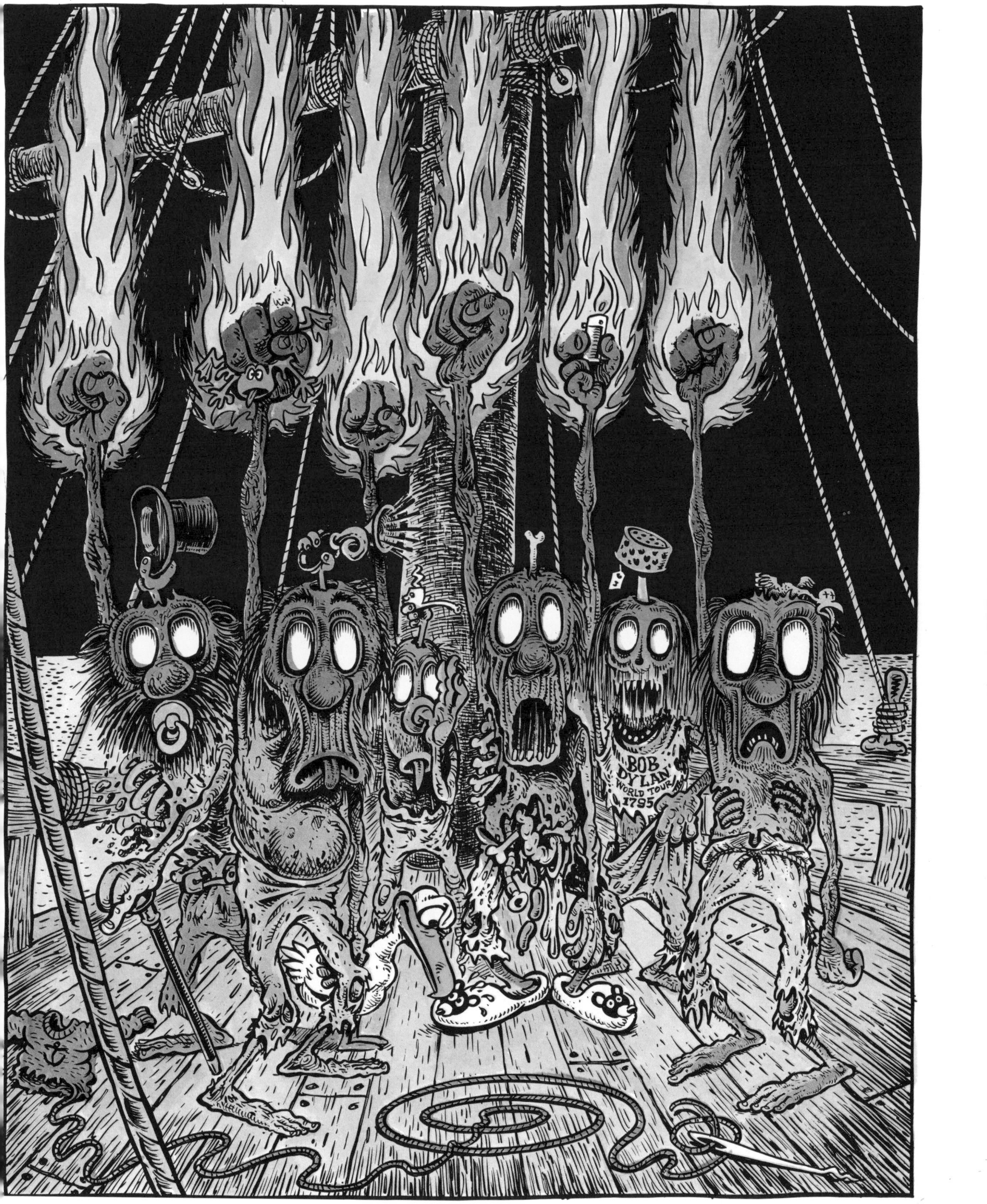
BOB DYLAN WORLD TOUR 1795

introduction

I had to read THE RIME OF THE ANCIENT MARINER when I was sixteen years old in high school in Houston, Texas. I could tell it was going to be hard to understand because I could barely make it through the title. Why couldn't this guy Coleridge call an old sailor an *old sailor*? And he obviously didn't even know how to spell 'rhyme'. As for the words in the poem itself, even the *teacher* didn't know what 'swound' meant. I can only imagine what difficulty kids in contemporary schools nowadays — which reputedly don't even teach literature any more, just computer science — might have with phrases like 'Nor any drop to drink', or 'Thorough the fog it came', or 'This is strange, I trow!'. Anyway, slowly and laboriously we inched our way through the iambic septemeter. How much easier it would have been if we had had this illustrated version you now hold in your hands! But alas, the year was 1956, and Hunt Emerson had not yet begun his cartooning career.

The gist of the poem, more or less, is this: an old sailor stops a man (one of three) on his way to a wedding party and forces him to listen to the story of how he, during a long sea trip which took him far enough south to get stuck in the ice, shoots with his crossbow for no reason at all the friendly albatross which had been following the ship and which may have been bringing, depending on the mood of the sailors, either good or bad luck. About this time the vessel enters the doldrums, the wind dies, and they run out of water. The other crewmen hang the dead albatross around our sailor's neck for laying this bad trip on them. Then all except him die of thirst. Things are looking pretty grim for our sailor when one night, as he stands on the deck among the corpses ('corses', as Coleridge calls them), watching the sea snakes, he senses for the first time the happiness and beauty of these formerly-despised serpents, and he starts sending out good vibes for a change, and suddenly his luck takes a turn for the better. It begins to rain, and the dead albatross drops from his neck. Spirits carry the boat homeward at tremendous speed, using the bodies of the dead seamen to man the rigging. Just as it reaches sight of shore, the ship sinks like lead. Our sailor is rescued by three astonished witnesses who row out and pluck him from the water, then flip out upon hearing his tale. He is thenceforth doomed to roam the earth retelling his story to whomever he can corner, reluctant listeners such as the wedding guest, whom he causes to miss the wedding party but who wakes up the next morning 'a sadder and a wiser man'.

One could perhaps say that the Coleridge poem is lacking in humour. Hunt Emerson has amply made up for that in this Crack Editions two hundredth (approximately) anniversary printing which is, incidentally, beautifully coloured by Carol Bennett of Knockabout. We sure could have used this back in Mrs Teshner's English class. Anyway, we managed to read the thing, but still no one understood it. (I was only partially gratified to discover, later, that no one of any era can agree what it is all about.) It might have helped stir up our interest if the teacher had told us that the author was an opium addict. That would probably have caught our attention for a minute or two, but she neglected to mention it.

Samuel Taylor Coleridge was born in Devonshire in southwest England in 1772, and is famous mainly for THE RIME OF THE ANCIENT MARINER and two other poems (*Kubla Khan* and *Christabel*) he wrote when he was young. He is described by his friends and contemporaries as an engaging non-stop talker whose discourse tended to wander from one subject to another, never returning to the original point. At age twenty-two he was involved in a project to form a utopian community, called Pantisocracy, to be organized on the banks of the Susquehanna River in America, but the plan failed for lack of funds. His poetic powers blossomed when William Wordsworth came to live near him in north Somerset in 1797. The two men published *Lyrical Ballads* and became the leaders of the English Romantic movement. Coleridge fell in love with Wordsworth's sister-in-law, although he was already married at the time. And as if his life weren't already complicated enough, he became addicted to opium.

In those days, it must be pointed out, not only was opium not illegal, but the very concept of drug addiction was unknown. Doctors prescribed it for everything from neurosis to intestinal disorders, and opium use was not considered a stigma until the middle of the 1800s, after which the careers of Coleridge and Thomas De Quincey (author of *The Opium Eater*) were held up in solemn warning as examples of how the drug leads to wretchedness and destruction. But Coleridge's career was not in fact destroyed. He lived to age 62 and continued to write poetry and criticism for the rest of his life. In non-English-speaking countries he is perhaps better known for his critical tome, *Biographia Literaria* (published in 1817), than for his poetry. Coleridge's physical condition was good enough that he often walked twenty to thirty miles a day. He referred to the discomfort of withdrawal symptoms from his addiction as 'atonic gout'.

Now I know that Coleridge used archaic words and spellings like 'kirk' and 'shrieve' to create a false look of antiquity. If I had known back in high school what I know now, with him using words like that on purpose just to make life miserable for me, I would have blown the whistle on him. I can imagine how long the Houston School Board would have wanted us to continue studying the works of a DRUG FIEND and a DOPE ADDICT. In the fifties, just like today, the right-wingers were already busy cleansing the school libraries of most literature written in the twentieth century ('modernism') and probably would have welcomed a chance to add the entire nineteenth century to their hit list.

The chapter heads at the beginning of each of the seven parts of this edition were added by Coleridge himself as marginal notes in later editions, to give the impression of the poem being interpreted by a more recent, but still ancient, scholar. The frontispiece of this edition illustrates the following verses, which appeared in the first 1797 edition of the poem (immediately before the appearance of the spirits in part the sixth).

I turned my head in fear and dread,
and by the Holy Rood
the bodies had avanc'd, and now
before the mast they stood!

They lifted up their stiff right arms,
they held them strait and tight . . .
and each right-arm burn't like a torch,
a torch that's borne upright! . . .
Their stony eye-balls glitter'd on
in the red and smoky light!

Curiously, Coleridge deleted these verses from later editions, as he seemed to think he was laying it on a little too thick. Hunt Emerson thought it was too good an image to waste, however, so he resurrected it for this edition.

Hunt Emerson is known not to use opium, or anything like it, so this edition is probably safe from censorship as long as Coleridge's name doesn't come up, which is unlikely. Hunt has, by the way, drawn himself into the story in a minor character role as a tidbit for future Coleridge scholars, if there is such a thing.

GILBERT SHELTON

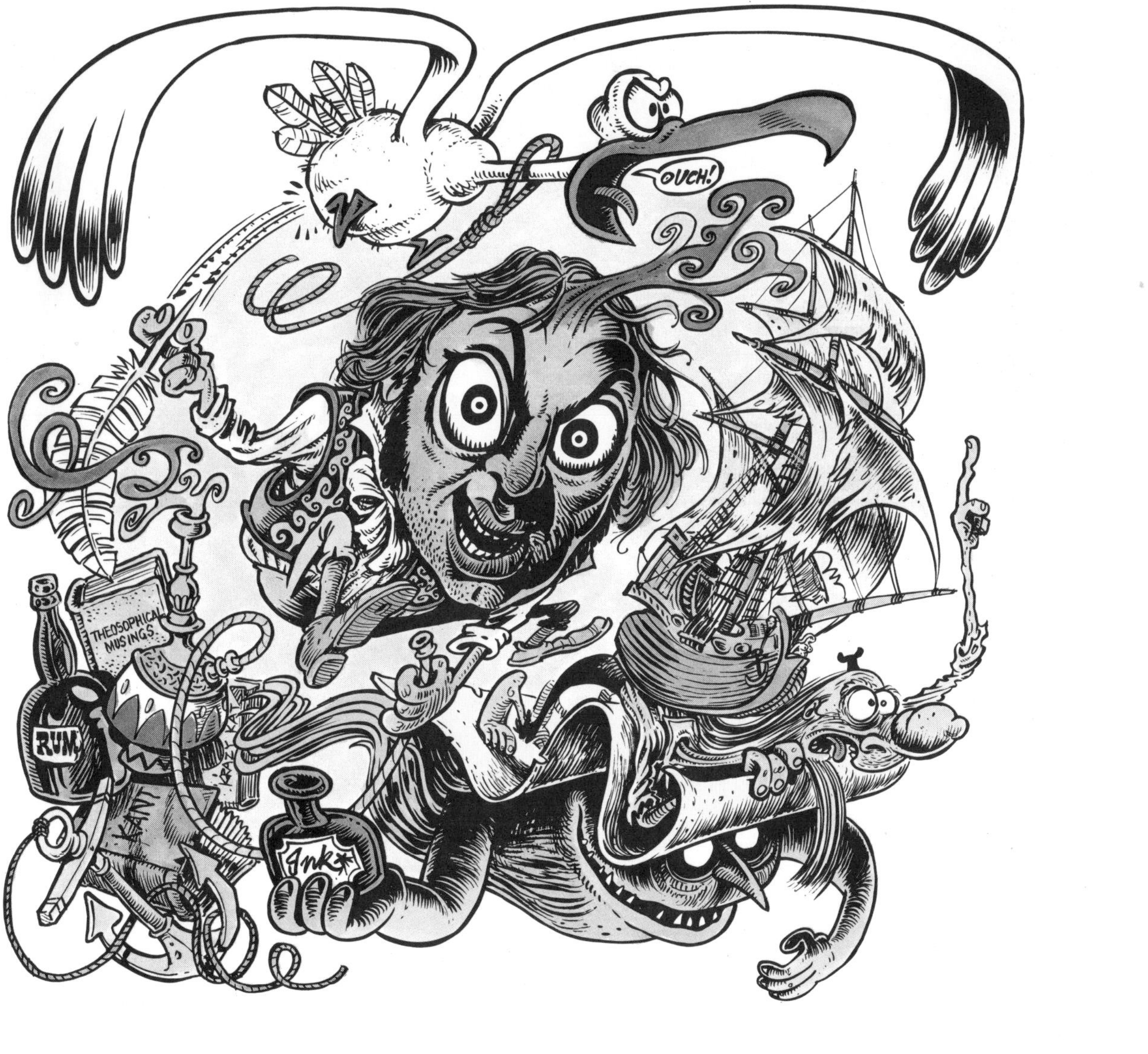
OUCH!
THEOSOPHICAL MUSINGS
RUM
Ink

part the first

An ancient Mariner meeteth three Gallants bidden to a wedding-feast, and detaineth one.

The Wedding-Guest is spellbound by the eye of the old sea-faring man, and constrained to hear his tale.

The Mariner tells how the ship sailed southward with a good wind and fair weather, till it reached the line.

The Wedding-Guest heareth the bridal music; but the Mariner continueth his tale.

The ship drawn by a storm toward the south pole.

The land of ice, and of fearful sounds, where no living thing was to be seen.

Till a great seabird, called the Albatross, came through the snow-fog, and was received with great joy and hospitality.

And lo! the Albatross proveth a bird of good omen, and followeth the ship as it returned northward through fog and floating ice.

The ancient Mariner inhospitably killeth the pious bird of good omen.

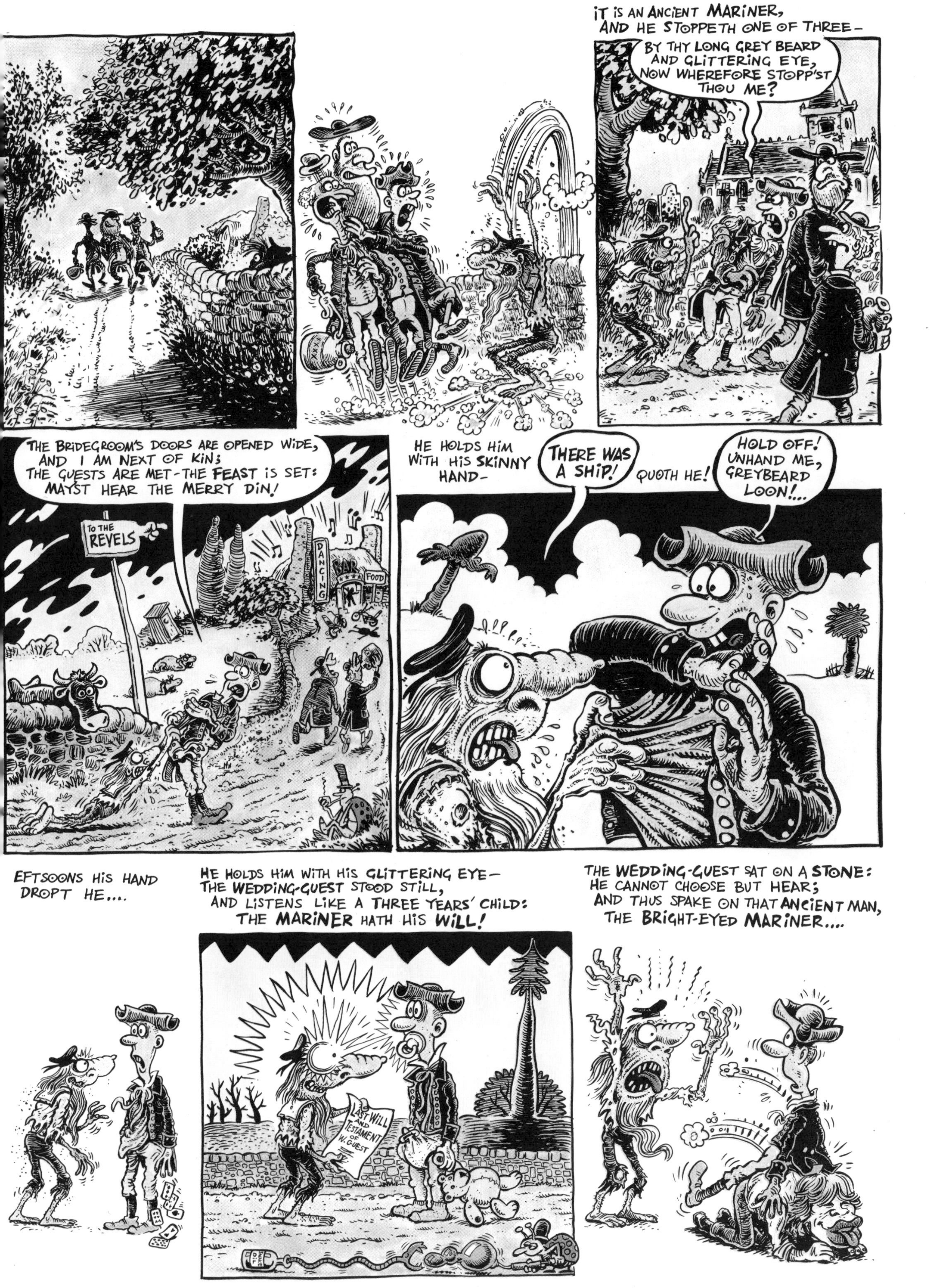

IT IS AN ANCIENT MARINER,
AND HE STOPPETH ONE OF THREE-
BY THY LONG GREY BEARD AND GLITTERING EYE, NOW WHEREFORE STOPP'ST THOU ME?
THE BRIDEGROOM'S DOORS ARE OPENED WIDE, AND I AM NEXT OF KIN; THE GUESTS ARE MET-THE FEAST IS SET: MAYST HEAR THE MERRY DIN!
TO THE REVELS
DANCING
BAR
FOOD
HE HOLDS HIM WITH HIS SKINNY HAND-
THERE WAS A SHIP!
QUOTH HE!
HOLD OFF! UNHAND ME, GREYBEARD LOON!...
EFTSOONS HIS HAND DROPT HE....
HE HOLDS HIM WITH HIS GLITTERING EYE-
THE WEDDING-GUEST STOOD STILL,
AND LISTENS LIKE A THREE YEARS' CHILD:
THE MARINER HATH HIS WILL!
LAST WILL AND TESTAMENT OF W. GUEST
THE WEDDING-GUEST SAT ON A STONE:
HE CANNOT CHOOSE BUT HEAR;
AND THUS SPAKE ON THAT ANCIENT MAN,
THE BRIGHT-EYED MARINER....

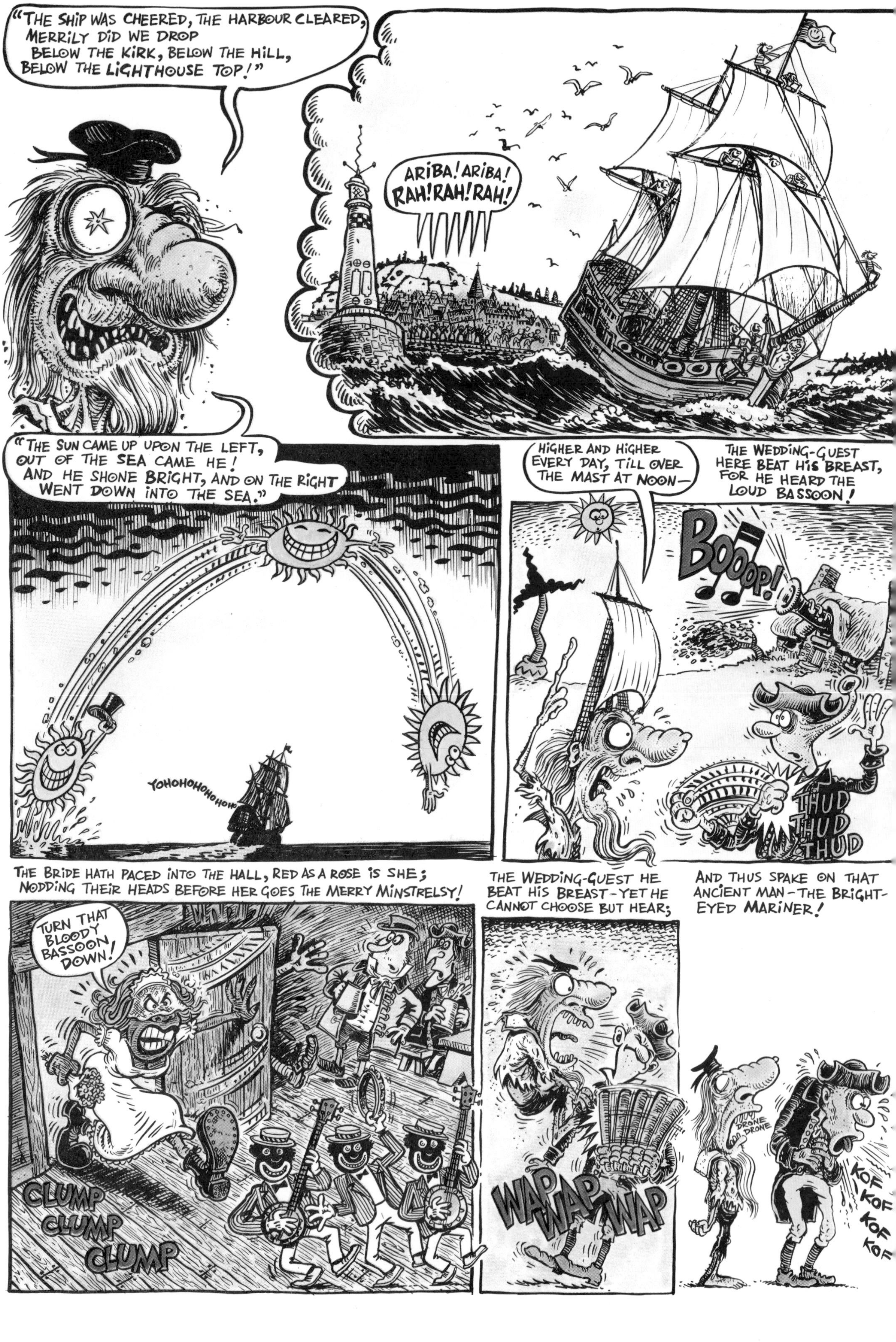

"THE SHIP WAS CHEERED, THE HARBOUR CLEARED, MERRILY DID WE DROP BELOW THE KIRK, BELOW THE HILL, BELOW THE LIGHTHOUSE TOP!"
ARIBA! ARIBA! RAH! RAH! RAH!
"THE SUN CAME UP UPON THE LEFT, OUT OF THE SEA CAME HE! AND HE SHONE BRIGHT, AND ON THE RIGHT WENT DOWN INTO THE SEA."
YOHOHOHOHOHOHO
HIGHER AND HIGHER EVERY DAY, TILL OVER THE MAST AT NOON—
THE WEDDING-GUEST HERE BEAT HIS BREAST, FOR HE HEARD THE LOUD BASSOON!
BOOOOP!
THUD THUD THUD
THE BRIDE HATH PACED INTO THE HALL, RED AS A ROSE IS SHE; NODDING THEIR HEADS BEFORE HER GOES THE MERRY MINSTRELSY!
TURN THAT BLOODY BASSOON DOWN!
CLUMP CLUMP CLUMP
THE WEDDING-GUEST HE BEAT HIS BREAST - YET HE CANNOT CHOOSE BUT HEAR;
WAP WAP WAP
AND THUS SPAKE ON THAT ANCIENT MAN - THE BRIGHT-EYED MARINER!
DRONE DRONE
KOF KOF KOF KOF

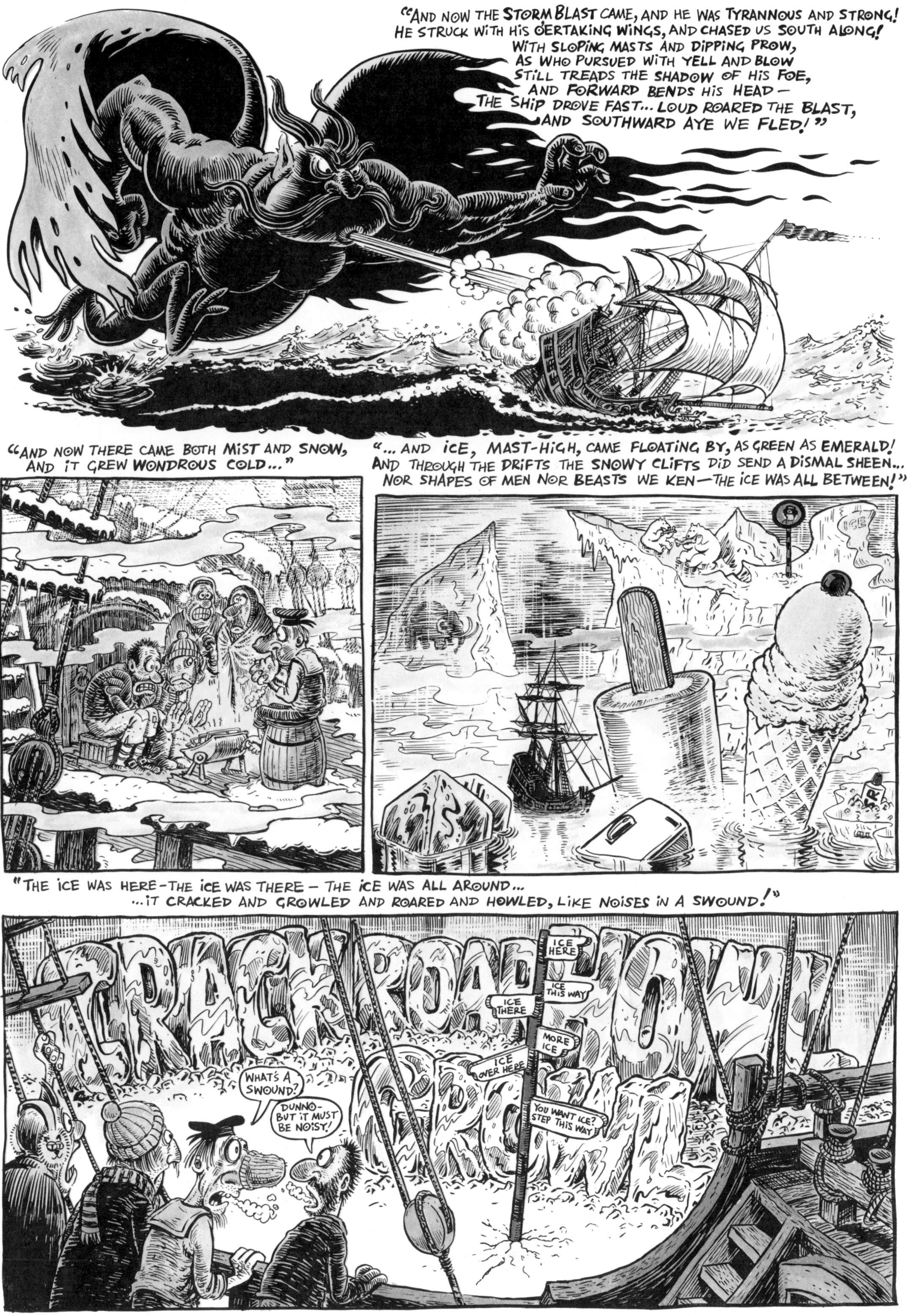
"AND NOW THE STORM BLAST CAME, AND HE WAS TYRANNOUS AND STRONG!
HE STRUCK WITH HIS O'ERTAKING WINGS, AND CHASED US SOUTH ALONG!
WITH SLOPING MASTS AND DIPPING PROW,
AS WHO PURSUED WITH YELL AND BLOW
STILL TREADS THE SHADOW OF HIS FOE,
AND FORWARD BENDS HIS HEAD—
THE SHIP DROVE FAST... LOUD ROARED THE BLAST,
AND SOUTHWARD AYE WE FLED!"
"AND NOW THERE CAME BOTH MIST AND SNOW, AND IT GREW WONDROUS COLD..."
"... AND ICE, MAST-HIGH, CAME FLOATING BY, AS GREEN AS EMERALD! AND THROUGH THE DRIFTS THE SNOWY CLIFTS DID SEND A DISMAL SHEEN... NOR SHAPES OF MEN NOR BEASTS WE KEN—THE ICE WAS ALL BETWEEN!"
ICE
"THE ICE WAS HERE-THE ICE WAS THERE – THE ICE WAS ALL AROUND...
...IT CRACKED AND GROWLED AND ROARED AND HOWLED, LIKE NOISES IN A SWOUND!"
ICE HERE
ICE THIS WAY
ICE THERE
MORE ICE
ICE OVER HERE
YOU WANT ICE? STEP THIS WAY
WHAT'S A SWOUND?
DUNNO- BUT IT MUST BE NOISY!

"At length did cross an **Albatross**....Thorough the Fog it came;
As if it had been a **Christian Soul**, we hailed it in **God's Name!**"

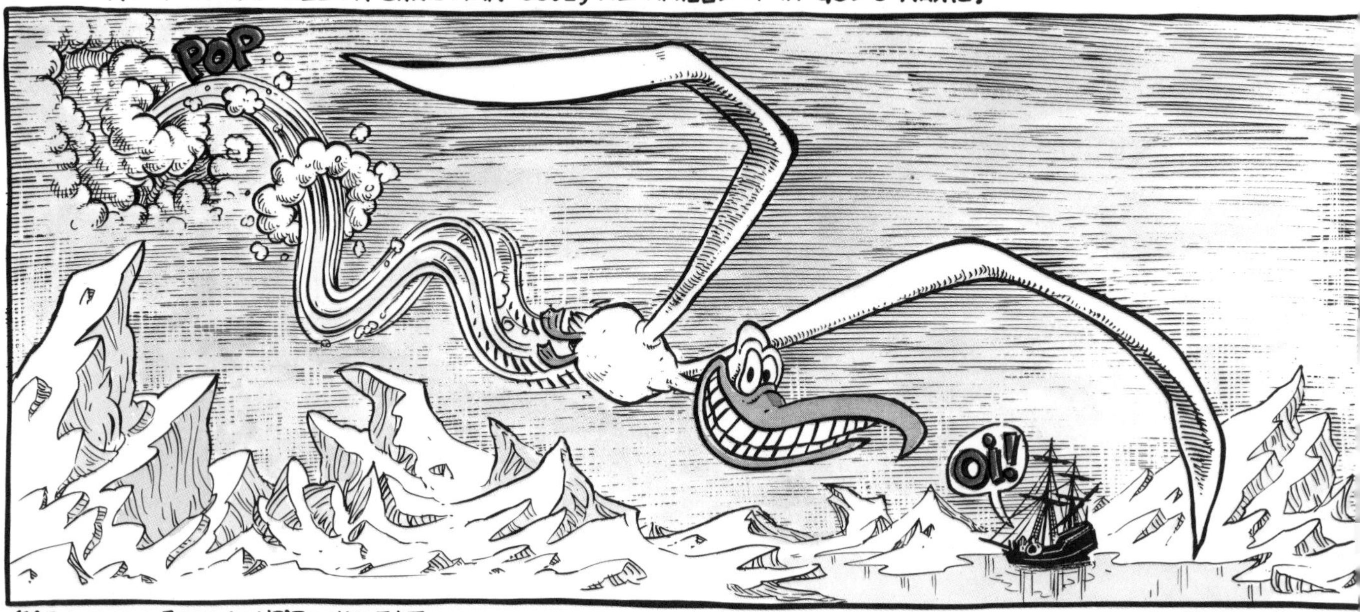
POP
Oi!

"It ate the **Food** it ne'er had eat.... ...and **Round** and **Round** it flew!"

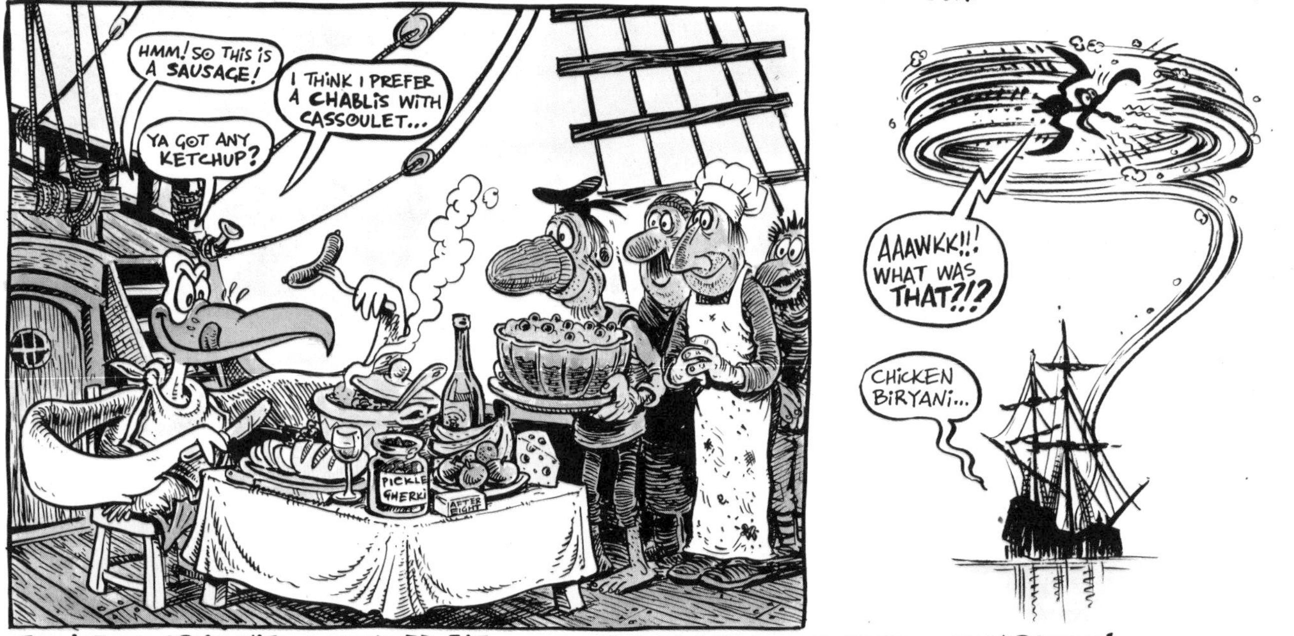
HMM! SO THIS IS A SAUSAGE!
YA GOT ANY KETCHUP?
I THINK I PREFER A CHABLIS WITH CASSOULET...
AAAWKK!! WHAT WAS THAT?!?
CHICKEN BIRYANI...

The **ice** did **split** with a **thunder-fit**... ...the **helmsman** steered us **through**!

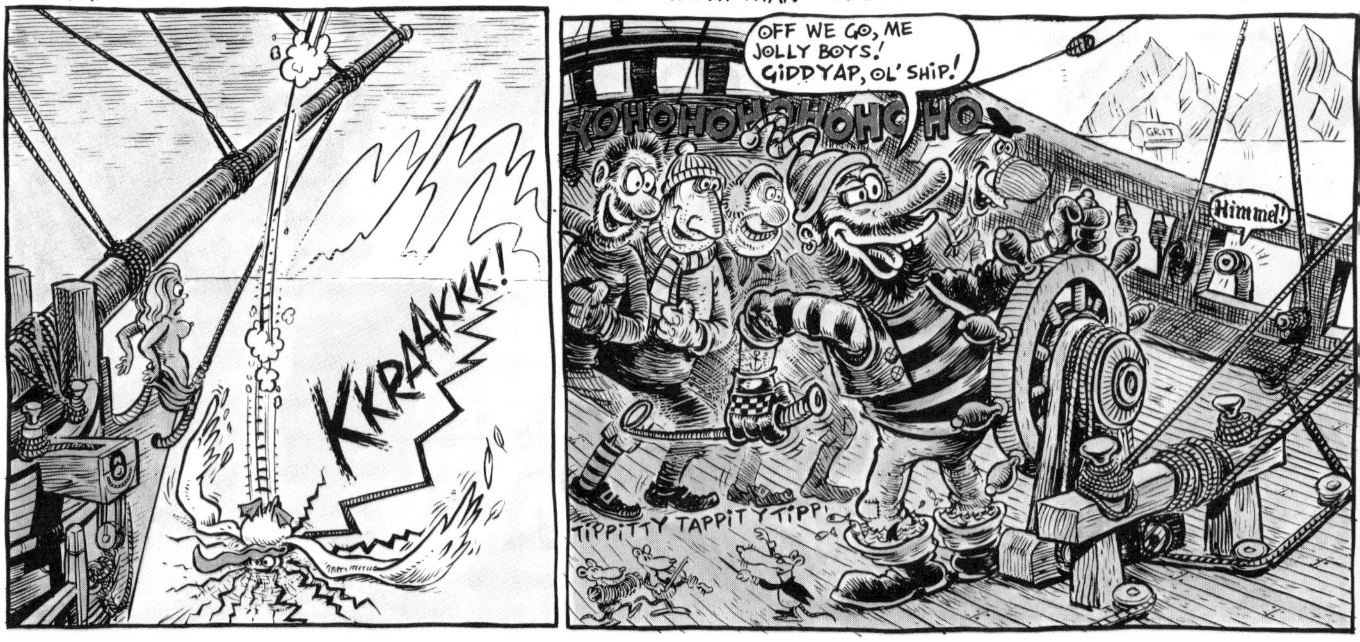
KKRAAKKK!
OFF WE GO, ME JOLLY BOYS! GIDDYAP, OL' SHIP!
YOHOHOHOHOHOHO HO
Himmel!
TIPPITTY TAPPITTY TIPP!

AND A GOOD SOUTH WIND SPRUNG UP BEHIND –
THE ALBATROSS DID FOLLOW....

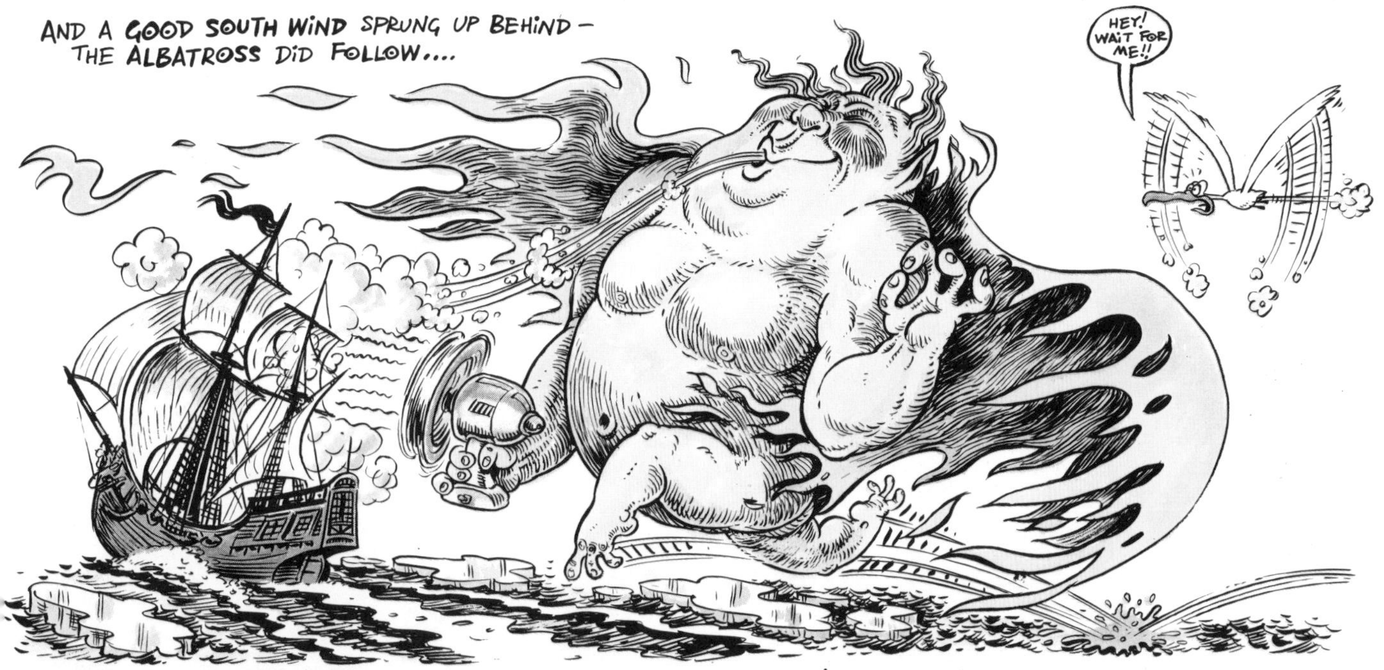
HEY! WAIT FOR ME!!

...AND EVERY DAY, FOR FOOD OR PLAY, CAME TO THE MARINER'S HOLLO!

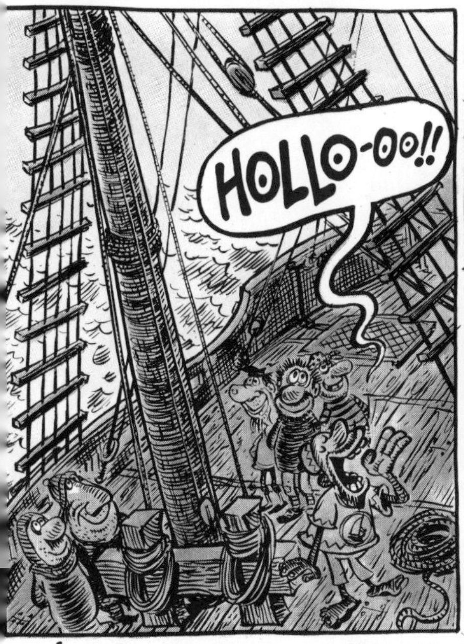
HOLLO-OO!!

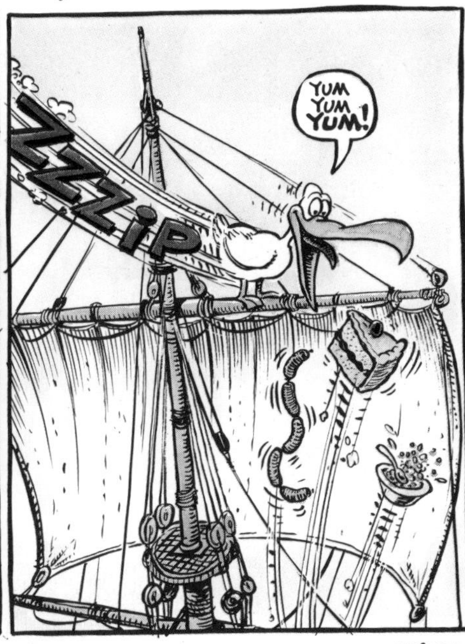
ZZZIP
YUM YUM YUM!

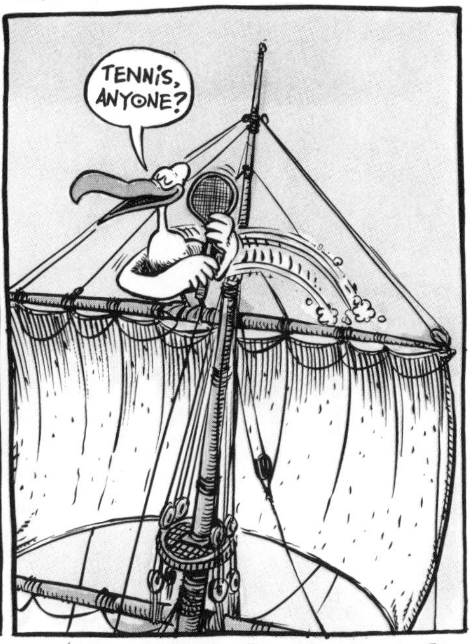
TENNIS, ANYONE?

IN MIST OR CLOUD, ON MAST OR SHROUD, IT PERCHED FOR VESPERS NINE...

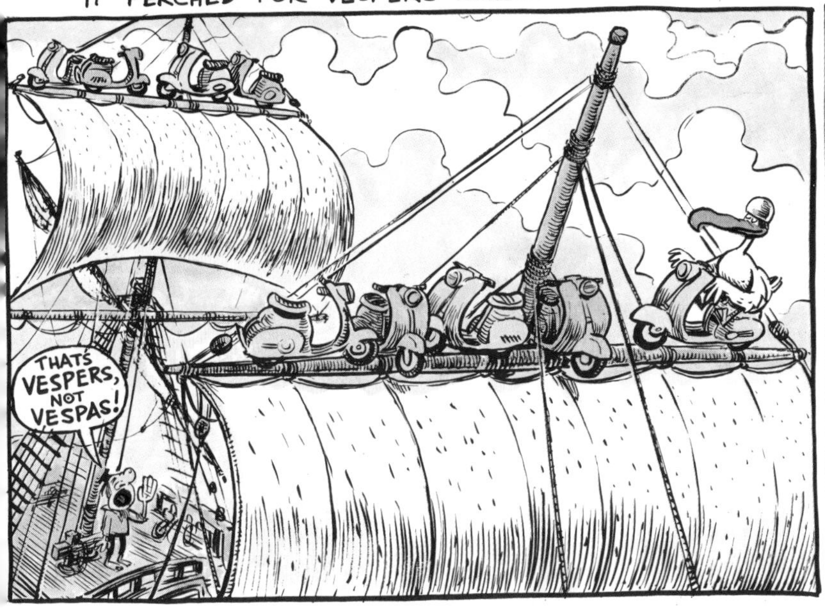
THAT'S VESPERS, NOT VESPAS!

...WHILES ALL THE NIGHT, THROUGH FOG-SMOKE WHITE, GLIMMERED THE WHITE MOONSHINE!

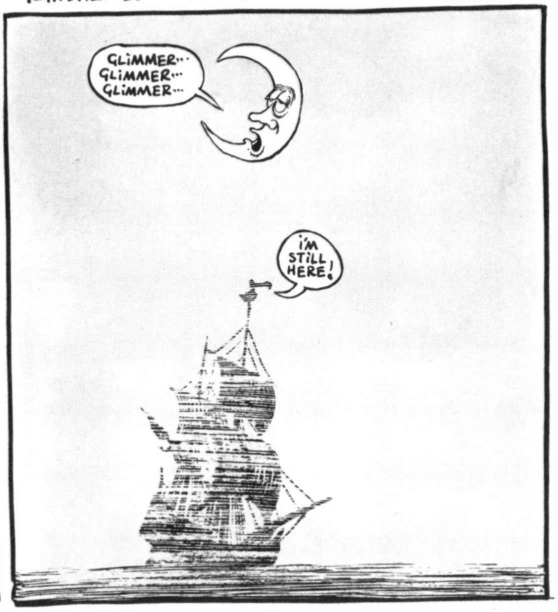
GLIMMER... GLIMMER... GLIMMER...
I'M STILL HERE!

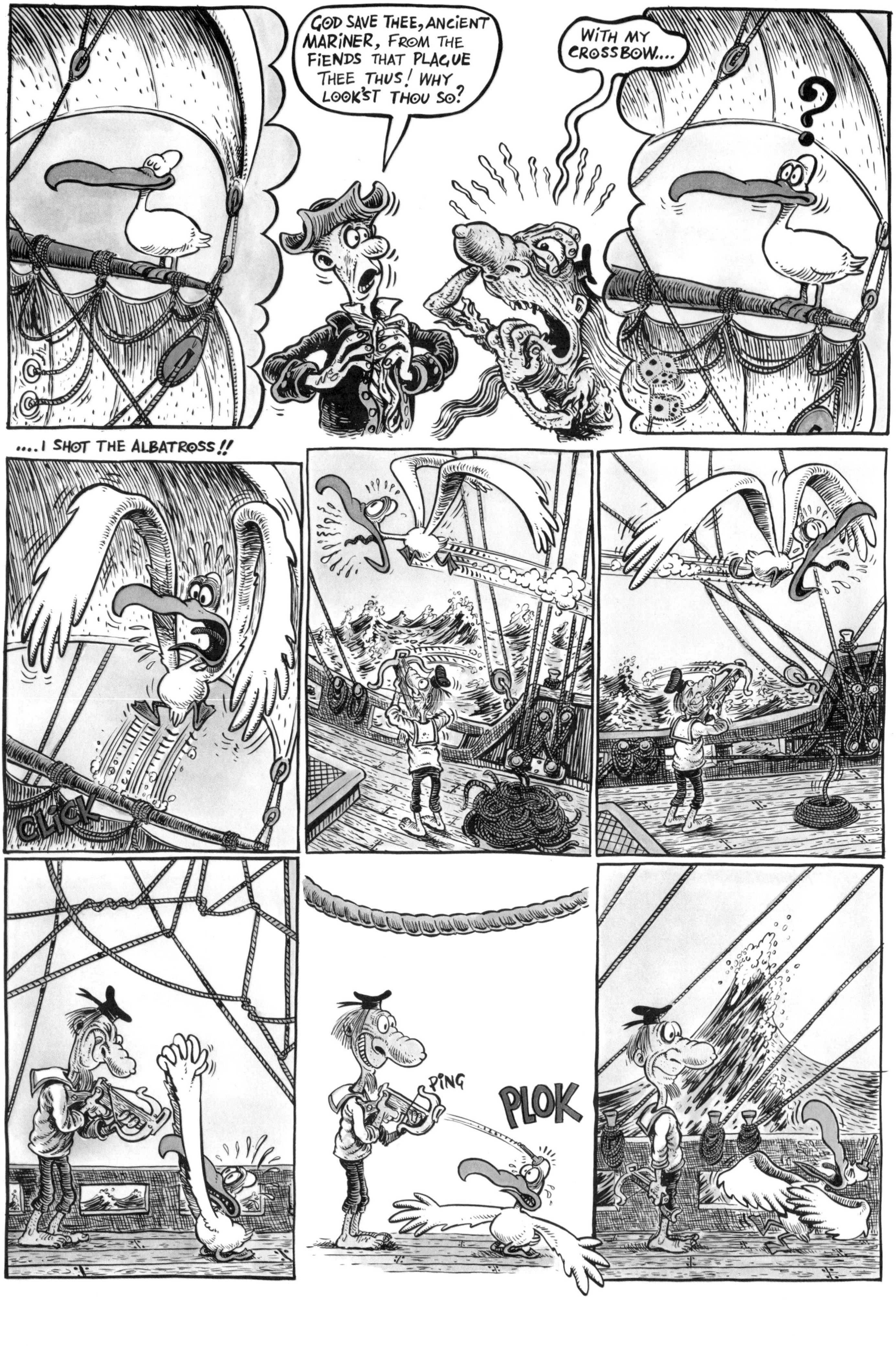

GOD SAVE THEE, ANCIENT MARINER, FROM THE FIENDS THAT PLAGUE THEE THUS! WHY LOOK'ST THOU SO?
WITH MY CROSSBOW....
?
....I SHOT THE ALBATROSS!!
CLICK
PING
PLOK

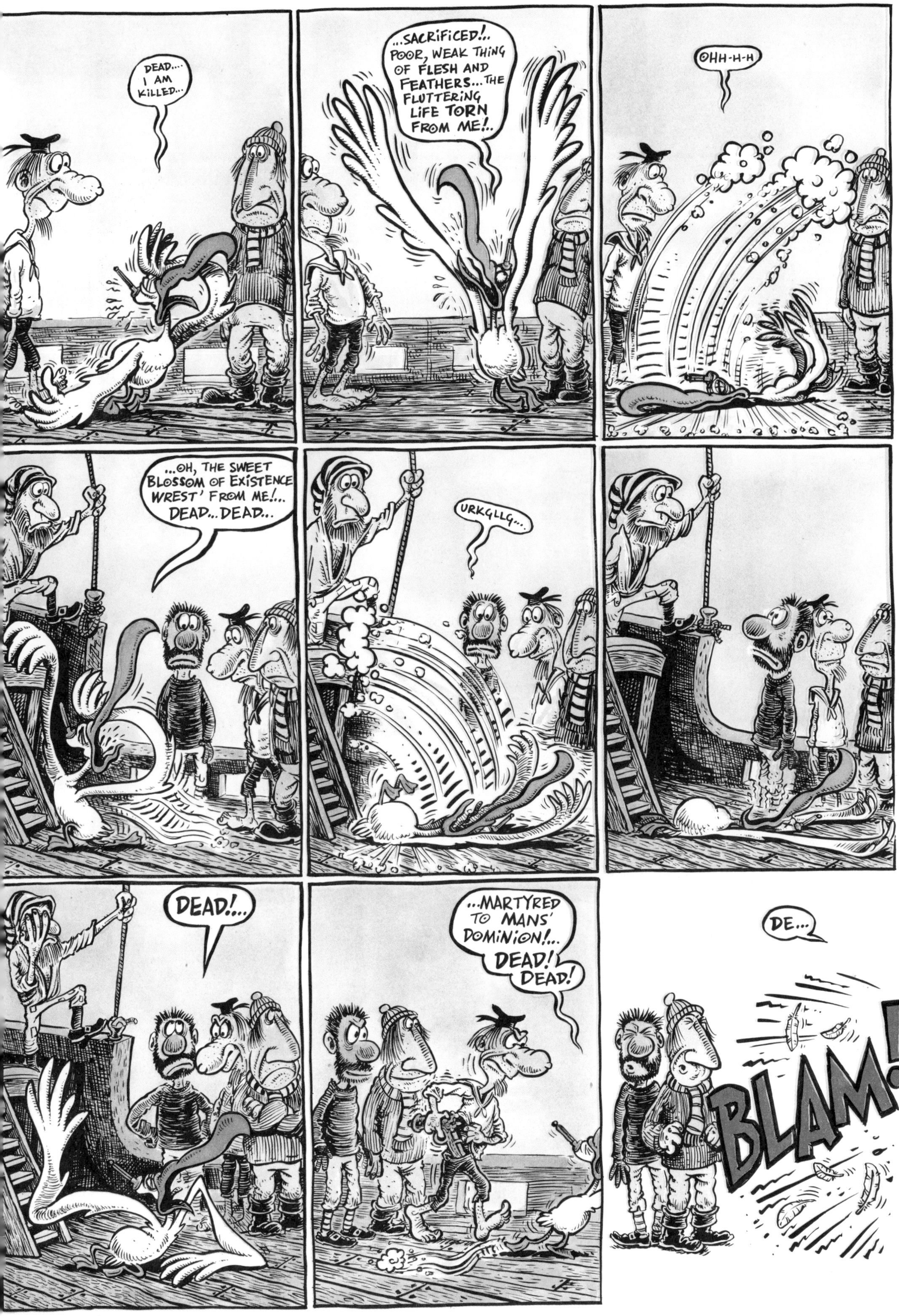
DEAD.... I AM KILLED...
...SACRIFICED!.. POOR, WEAK THING OF FLESH AND FEATHERS... THE FLUTTERING LIFE TORN FROM ME!..
OHH-H-H
...OH, THE SWEET BLOSSOM OF EXISTENCE WREST' FROM ME!... DEAD...DEAD...
URKGLLG...
DEAD!...
...MARTYRED TO MANS' DOMINION!... DEAD! DEAD!
DE...
BLAM!

part the second

His shipmates cry out against the ancient Mariner, for killing the bird of good luck.

But when the fog cleared off, they justify the same, and thus make themselves accomplices in the crime.

The fair breeze continues; the ship enters the Pacific Ocean, and sails northward,
even till it reaches the line.

The ship hath been suddenly becalmed.

And the Albatross begins to be avenged.

A spirit had followed them; one of the invisible inhabitants of this planet, neither departed souls nor angels; concerning whom the learned Jew, Josephus, and the Platonic Constantinopolitan, Michael Psellus, may be consulted. They are very numerous, and there is no climate or element without one or more. The shipmates, in their sore distress, would fain throw the whole guilt on the ancient Mariner: in sign whereof they hang the dead sea-bird round his neck.

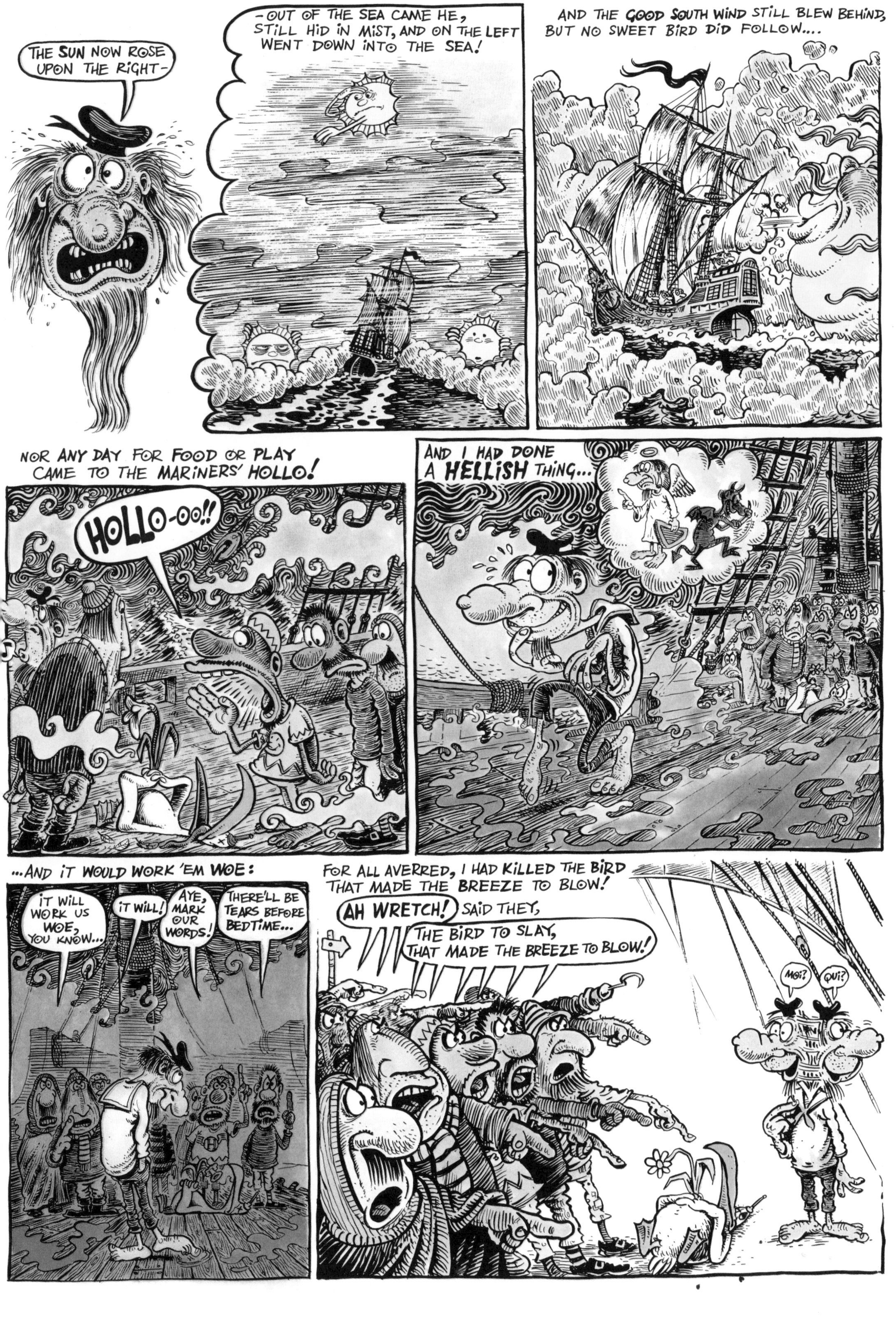
THE SUN NOW ROSE UPON THE RIGHT-
-OUT OF THE SEA CAME HE, STILL HID IN MIST, AND ON THE LEFT WENT DOWN INTO THE SEA!
AND THE GOOD SOUTH WIND STILL BLEW BEHIND, BUT NO SWEET BIRD DID FOLLOW....
NOR ANY DAY FOR FOOD OR PLAY CAME TO THE MARINERS' HOLLO!
HOLLO-OO!!
AND I HAD DONE A HELLISH THING...
...AND IT WOULD WORK 'EM WOE:
IT WILL WORK US WOE, YOU KNOW...
IT WILL!
AYE, MARK OUR WORDS!
THERE'LL BE TEARS BEFORE BEDTIME...
FOR ALL AVERRED, I HAD KILLED THE BIRD THAT MADE THE BREEZE TO BLOW!
AH WRETCH! SAID THEY,
THE BIRD TO SLAY, THAT MADE THE BREEZE TO BLOW!
MOI?
QUI?

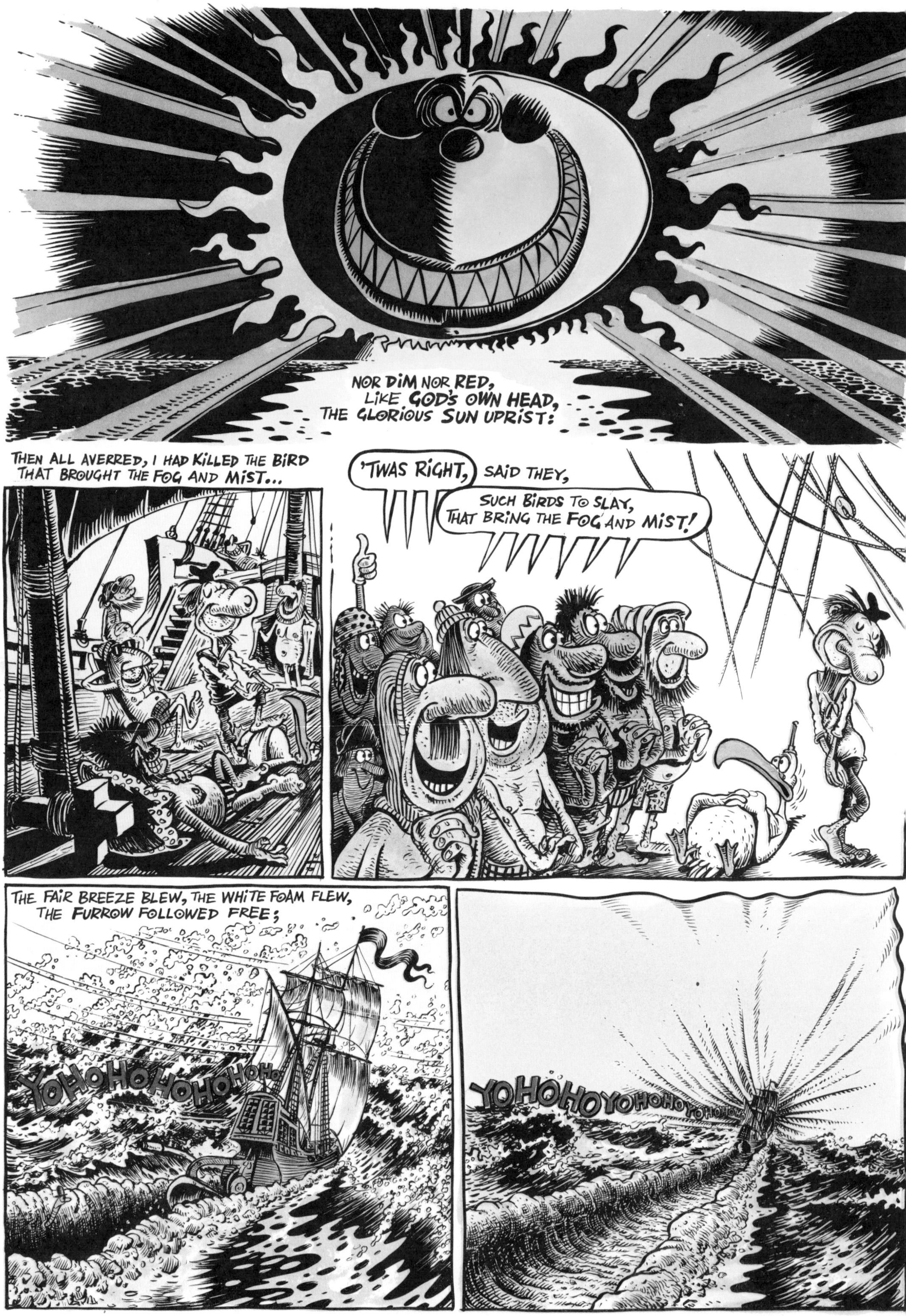

NOR DIM NOR RED,
LIKE GOD'S OWN HEAD,
THE GLORIOUS SUN UPRIST:
THEN ALL AVERRED, I HAD KILLED THE BIRD
THAT BROUGHT THE FOG AND MIST...
'TWAS RIGHT,
SAID THEY,
SUCH BIRDS TO SLAY,
THAT BRING THE FOG AND MIST!
THE FAIR BREEZE BLEW, THE WHITE FOAM FLEW,
THE FURROW FOLLOWED FREE;
YOHOHOHOHOHOHOHOHO
YOHOHOYOHOHOHOYOHOHOHO

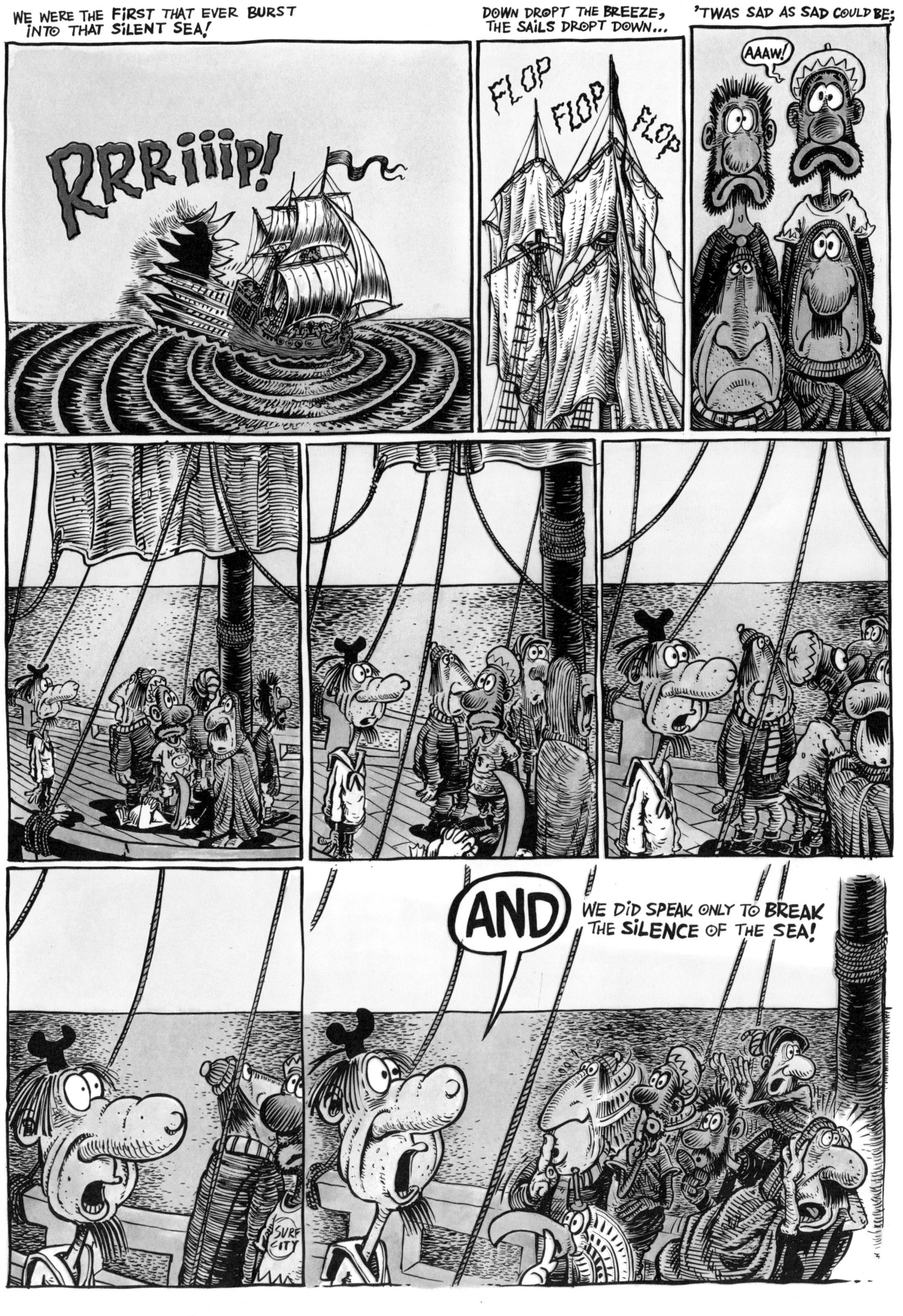
WE WERE THE FIRST THAT EVER BURST INTO THAT SILENT SEA!
RRRiiiP!
DOWN DROPT THE BREEZE, THE SAILS DROPT DOWN...
FLOP
FLOP
FLOP
'TWAS SAD AS SAD COULD BE;
AAAW!
SURF CITY
AND
WE DID SPEAK ONLY TO BREAK THE SILENCE OF THE SEA!

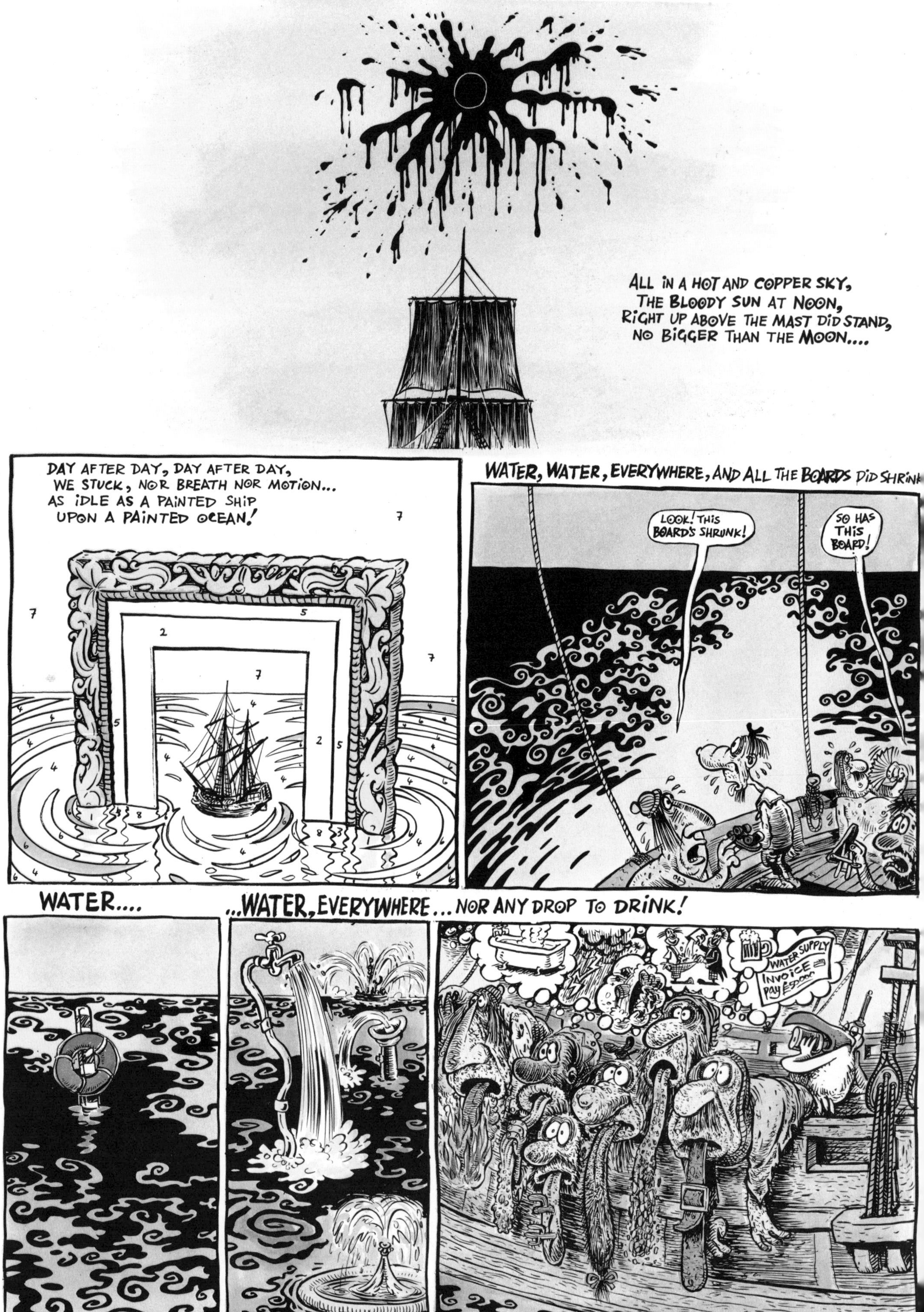
ALL IN A HOT AND COPPER SKY,
THE BLOODY SUN AT NOON,
RIGHT UP ABOVE THE MAST DID STAND,
NO BIGGER THAN THE MOON....
DAY AFTER DAY, DAY AFTER DAY,
WE STUCK, NOR BREATH NOR MOTION...
AS IDLE AS A PAINTED SHIP
UPON A PAINTED OCEAN!
7
7
5
2
7
7
WATER, WATER, EVERYWHERE, AND ALL THE BOARDS DID SHRINK
LOOK! THIS BOARD'S SHRUNK!
SO HAS THIS BOARD!
WATER....
...WATER, EVERYWHERE... NOR ANY DROP TO DRINK!
WATER SUPPLY
INVOICE
PAY £5000

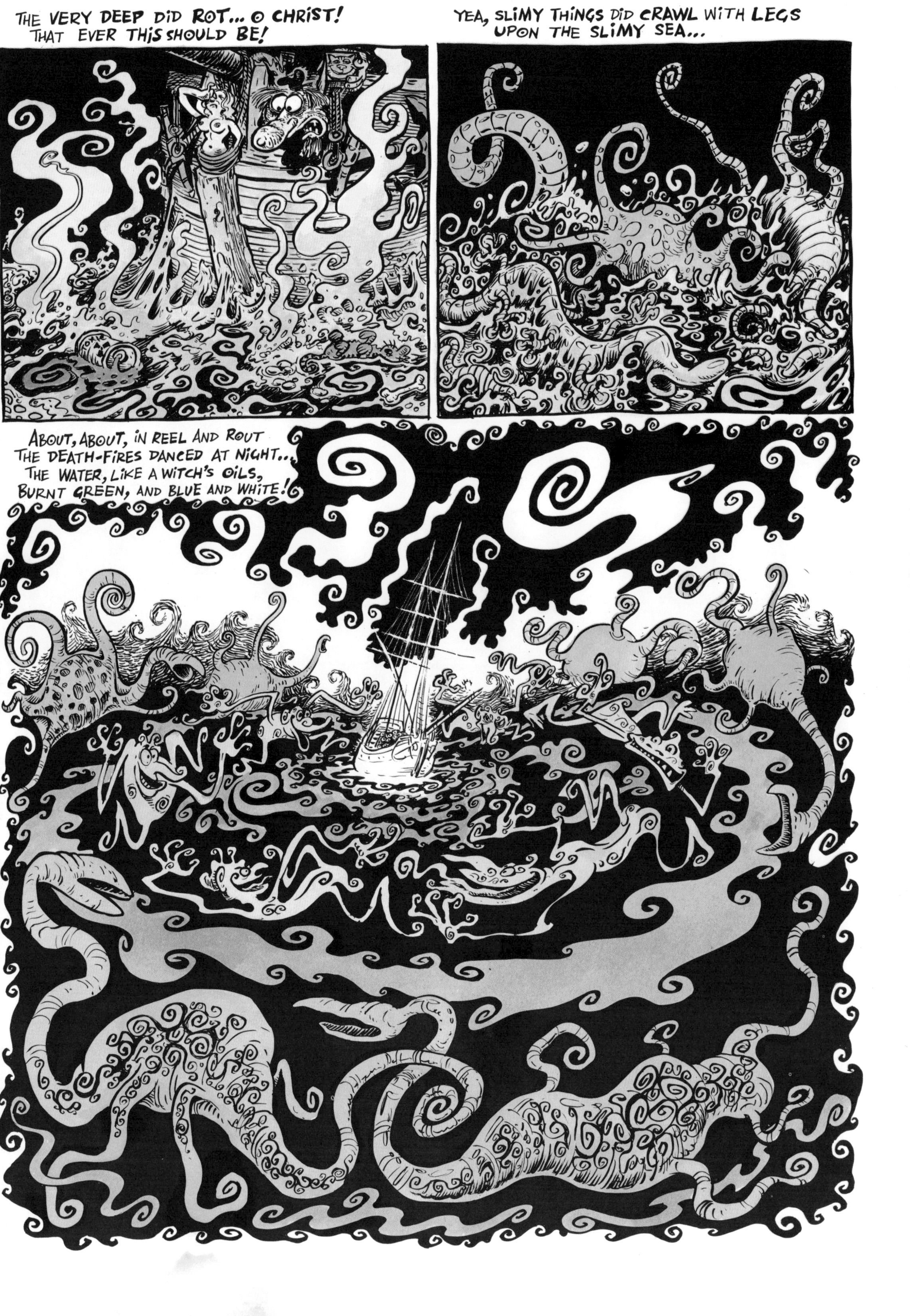
THE VERY DEEP DID ROT... O CHRIST! THAT EVER THIS SHOULD BE!
YEA, SLIMY THINGS DID CRAWL WITH LEGS UPON THE SLIMY SEA...
ABOUT, ABOUT, IN REEL AND ROUT THE DEATH-FIRES DANCED AT NIGHT... THE WATER, LIKE A WITCH'S OILS, BURNT GREEN, AND BLUE AND WHITE!

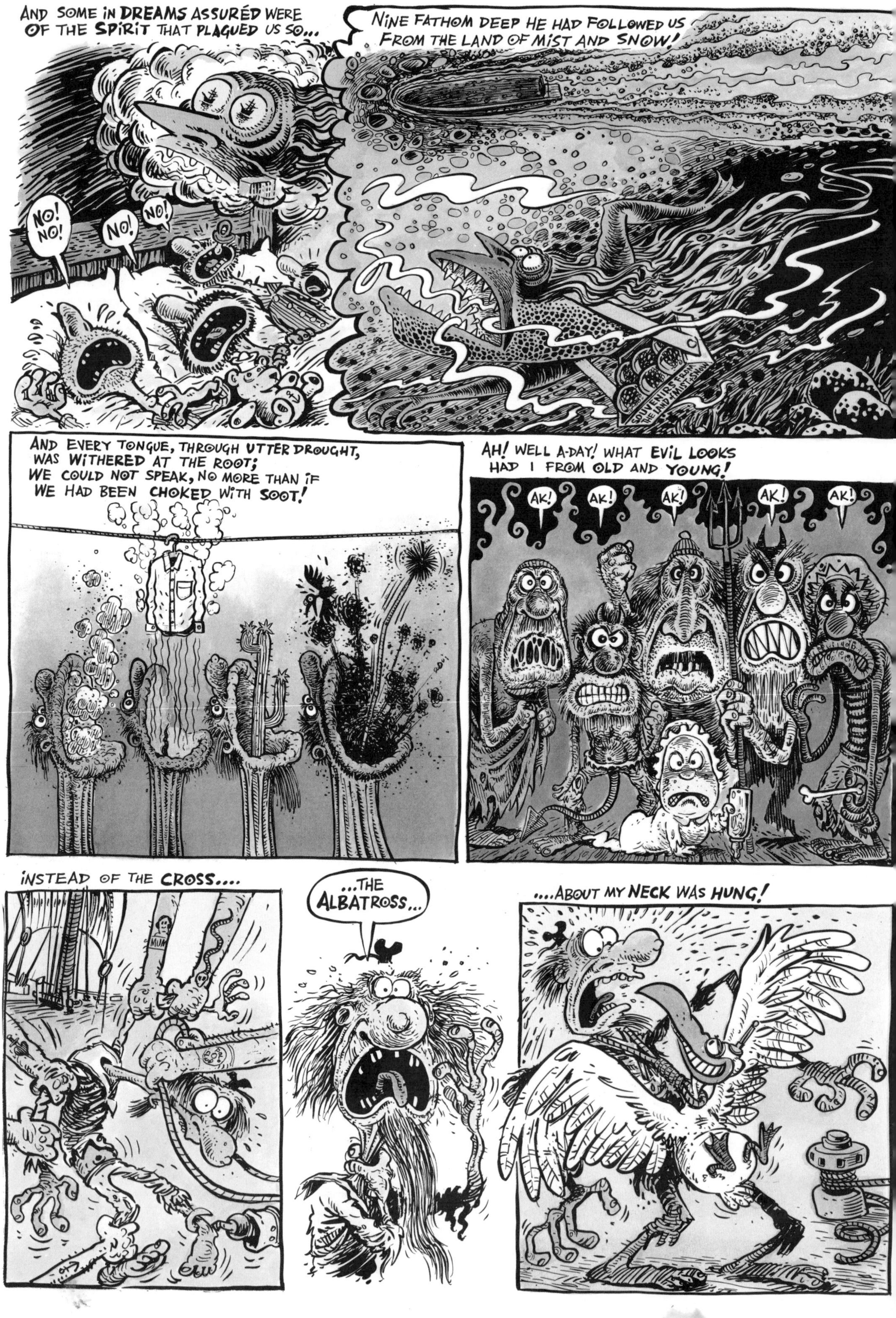
AND SOME IN DREAMS ASSURÉD WERE OF THE SPIRIT THAT PLAGUED US SO...
NO! NO!
NO!
NO!
NINE FATHOM DEEP HE HAD FOLLOWED US FROM THE LAND OF MIST AND SNOW!
AND EVERY TONGUE, THROUGH UTTER DROUGHT, WAS WITHERED AT THE ROOT; WE COULD NOT SPEAK, NO MORE THAN IF WE HAD BEEN CHOKED WITH SOOT!
AH! WELL A-DAY! WHAT EVIL LOOKS HAD I FROM OLD AND YOUNG!
AK!
AK!
AK!
AK!
AK!
INSTEAD OF THE CROSS....
...THE ALBATROSS...
....ABOUT MY NECK WAS HUNG!

part the third

The ancient Mariner beholdeth a sign in the element afar off.

At its nearer approach, it seemeth to him to be a ship; and at a dear ransom he freeth his speech from the bonds of thirst.

A flash of joy;

And horror follows. For can it be a ship that comes onward without wind or tide?

It seemeth him but the skeleton of a ship.

And its ribs are seen as bars on the face of the setting Sun. The Spectre-Woman and her Death-mate, and no other, on board the skeleton-ship.

Like vessel, like crew!

DEATH and LIFE-IN-DEATH have diced for the ship's crew, and she (the latter) winneth the ancient Mariner.

No twilight within the courts of the Sun.

At the rising of the Moon,
One after another,
His shipmates drop down dead;
But LIFE-IN-DEATH begins her work
on the ancient Mariner.

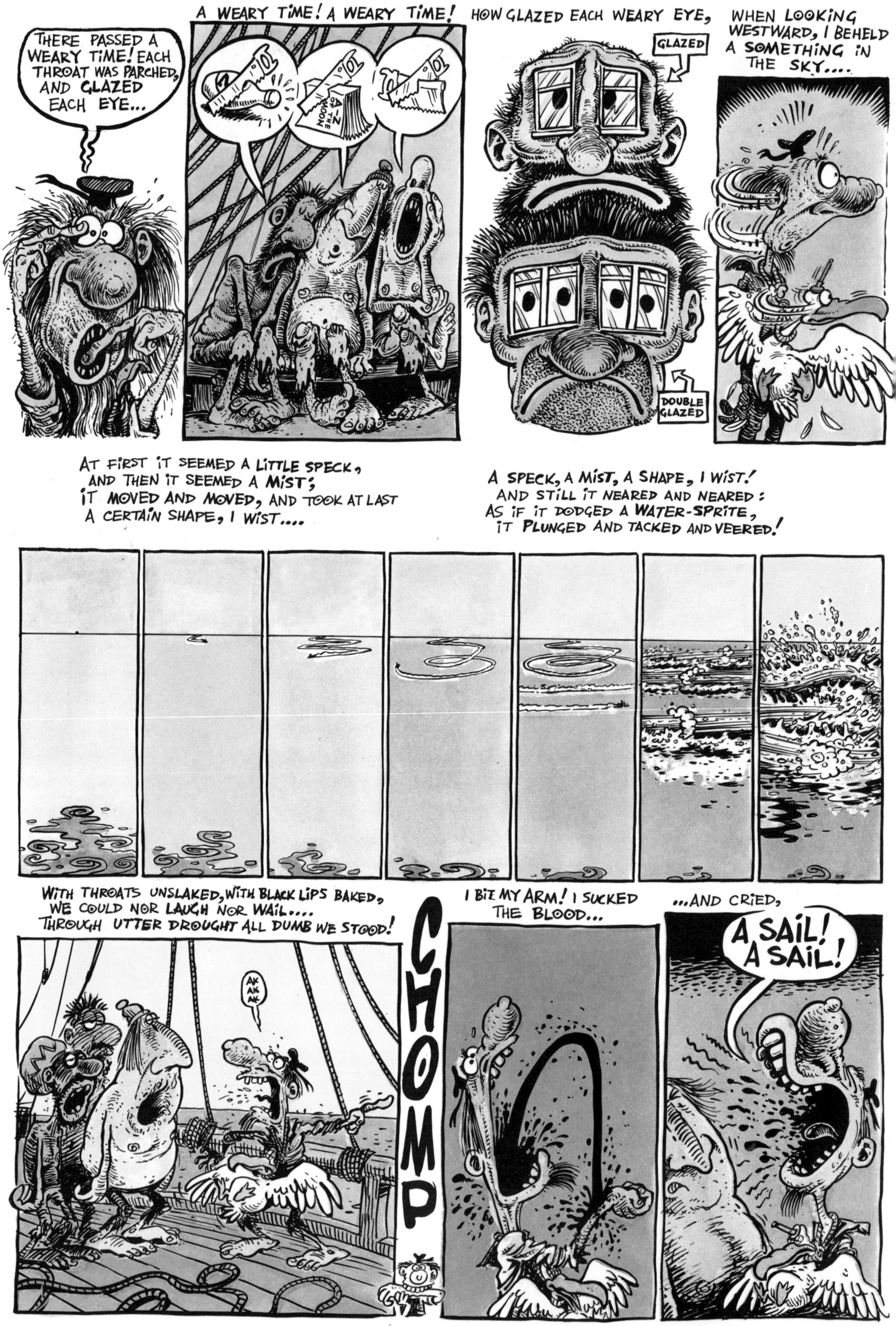
THERE PASSED A WEARY TIME! EACH THROAT WAS PARCHED, AND GLAZED EACH EYE...
A WEARY TIME! A WEARY TIME!
HOW GLAZED EACH WEARY EYE,
GLAZED
DOUBLE GLAZED
WHEN LOOKING WESTWARD, I BEHELD A SOMETHING IN THE SKY....
AT FIRST IT SEEMED A LITTLE SPECK, AND THEN IT SEEMED A MIST; IT MOVED AND MOVED, AND TOOK AT LAST A CERTAIN SHAPE, I WIST....
A SPECK, A MIST, A SHAPE, I WIST! AND STILL IT NEARED AND NEARED: AS IF IT DODGED A WATER-SPRITE, IT PLUNGED AND TACKED AND VEERED!
WITH THROATS UNSLAKED, WITH BLACK LIPS BAKED, WE COULD NOR LAUGH NOR WAIL.... THROUGH UTTER DROUGHT ALL DUMB WE STOOD!
AK AK AK
CHOMP
I BIT MY ARM! I SUCKED THE BLOOD...
...AND CRIED,
A SAIL! A SAIL!

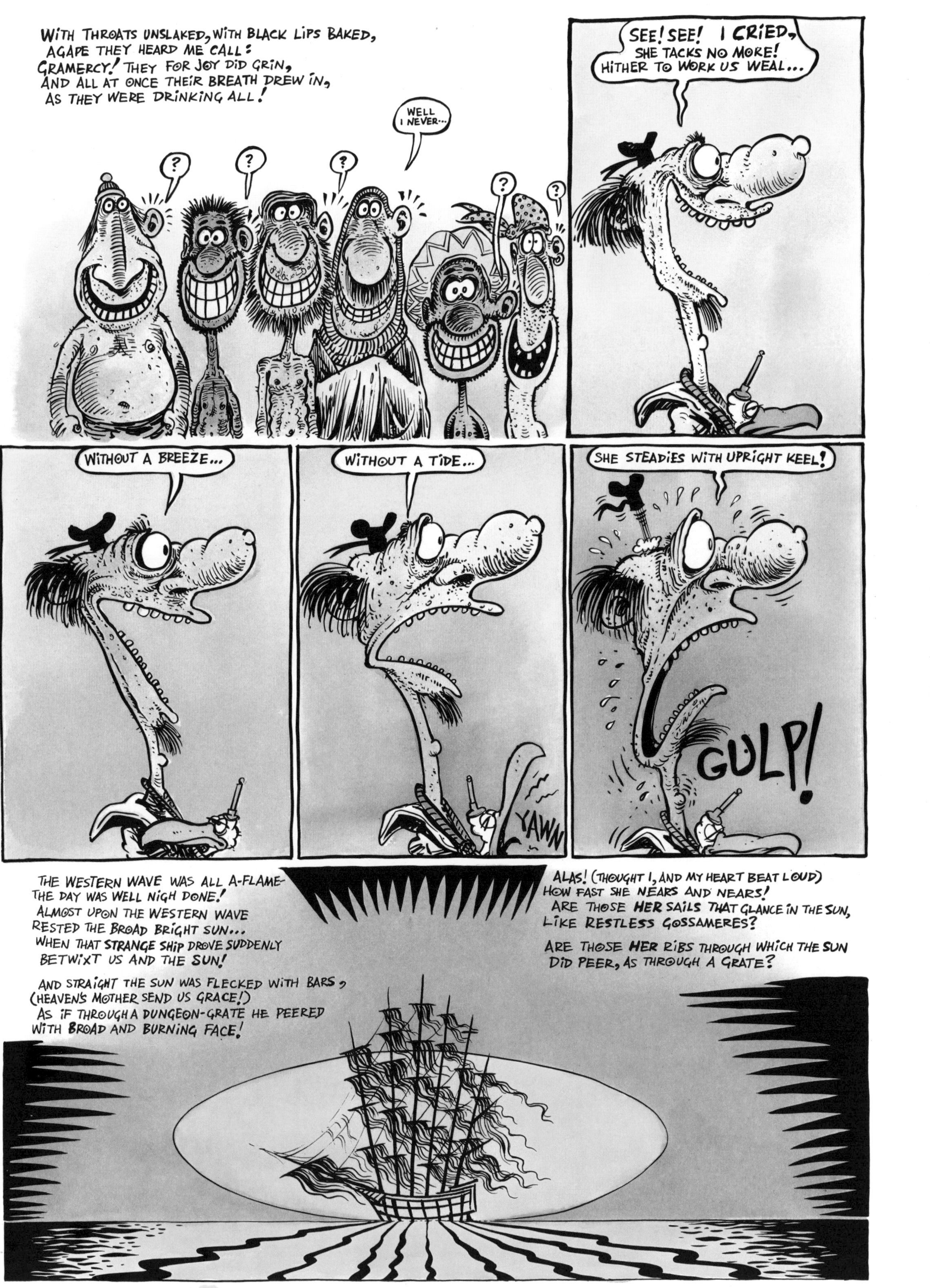

WITH THROATS UNSLAKED, WITH BLACK LIPS BAKED,
AGAPE THEY HEARD ME CALL:
GRAMERCY! THEY FOR JOY DID GRIN,
AND ALL AT ONCE THEIR BREATH DREW IN,
AS THEY WERE DRINKING ALL!
WELL I NEVER...
SEE! SEE! I CRIED, SHE TACKS NO MORE! HITHER TO WORK US WEAL...
WITHOUT A BREEZE...
WITHOUT A TIDE...
YAWN
SHE STEADIES WITH UPRIGHT KEEL!
GULP!
THE WESTERN WAVE WAS ALL A-FLAME
THE DAY WAS WELL NIGH DONE!
ALMOST UPON THE WESTERN WAVE
RESTED THE BROAD BRIGHT SUN...
WHEN THAT STRANGE SHIP DROVE SUDDENLY
BETWIXT US AND THE SUN!
AND STRAIGHT THE SUN WAS FLECKED WITH BARS,
(HEAVEN'S MOTHER SEND US GRACE!)
AS IF THROUGH A DUNGEON-GRATE HE PEERED
WITH BROAD AND BURNING FACE!
ALAS! (THOUGHT I, AND MY HEART BEAT LOUD)
HOW FAST SHE NEARS AND NEARS!
ARE THOSE HER SAILS THAT GLANCE IN THE SUN,
LIKE RESTLESS GOSSAMERES?
ARE THOSE HER RIBS THROUGH WHICH THE SUN
DID PEER, AS THROUGH A GRATE?

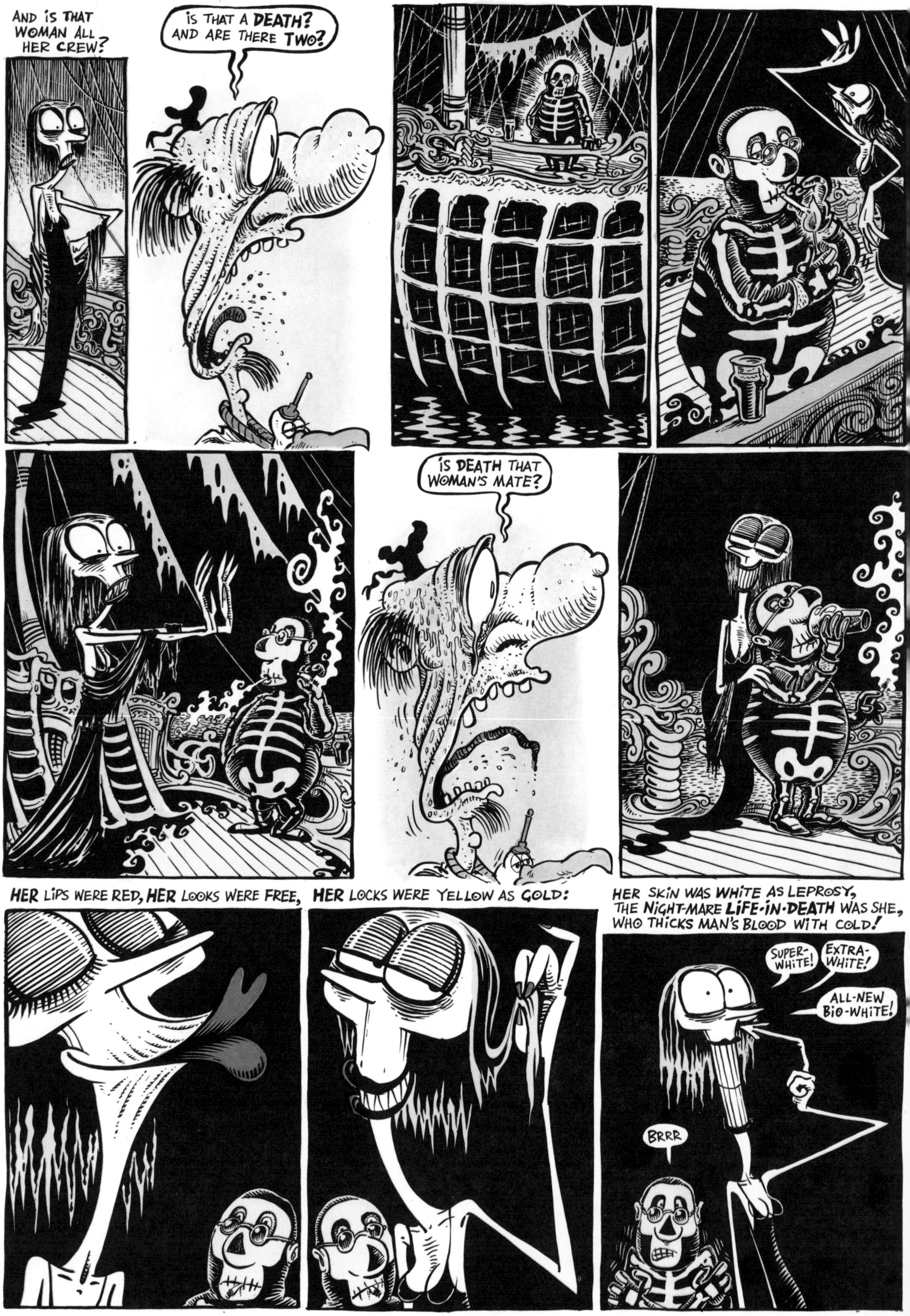
AND IS THAT WOMAN ALL HER CREW?
IS THAT A DEATH? AND ARE THERE TWO?
IS DEATH THAT WOMAN'S MATE?
HER LIPS WERE RED, HER LOOKS WERE FREE,
HER LOCKS WERE YELLOW AS GOLD:
HER SKIN WAS WHITE AS LEPROSY, THE NIGHT-MARE LIFE-IN-DEATH WAS SHE, WHO THICKS MAN'S BLOOD WITH COLD!
SUPER-WHITE!
EXTRA-WHITE!
ALL-NEW BIO-WHITE!
BRRR

THE NAKED HULK ALONGSIDE CAME,
AND THE TWAIN WERE CASTING DICE;

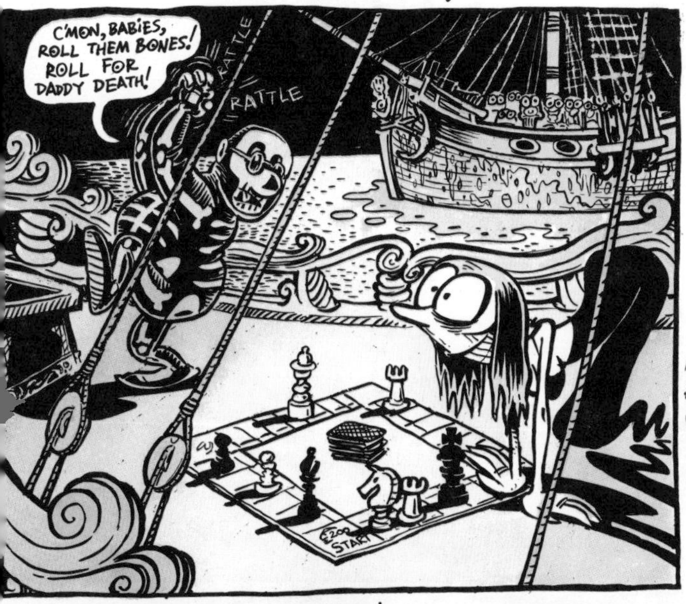
C'MON, BABIES, ROLL THEM BONES! ROLL FOR DADDY DEATH!
RATTLE
RATTLE
£200
START

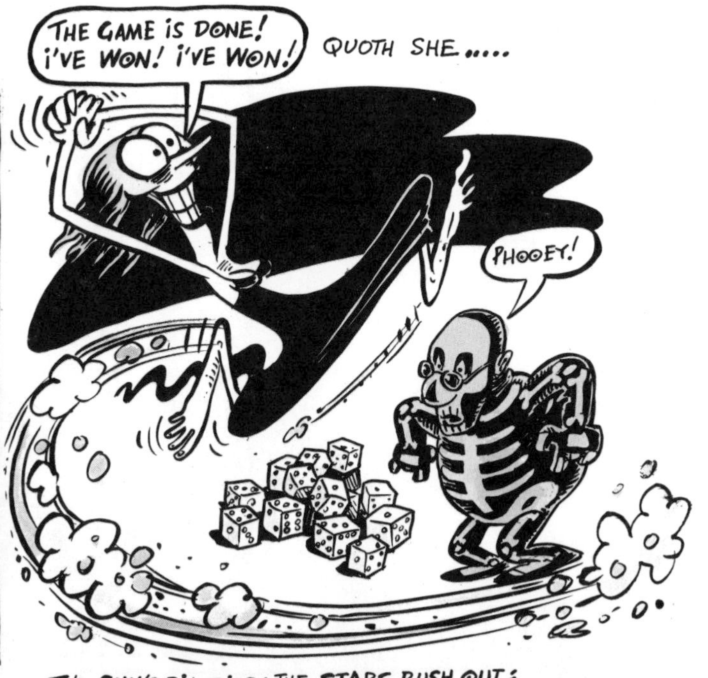
THE GAME IS DONE! I'VE WON! I'VE WON!
PHOOEY!

QUOTH SHE.....

....AND WHISTLES THRICE!

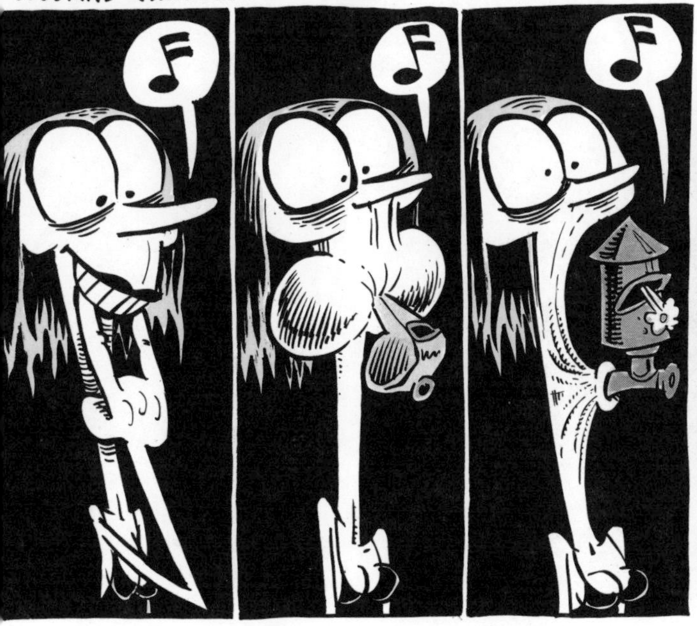

THE SUN'S RIM DIPS; THE STARS RUSH OUT:
AT ONE STRIDE COMES THE DARK;
WITH FAR-HEARD WHISPER, O'ER THE SEA,
OFF SHOT THE SPECTRE-BARK!

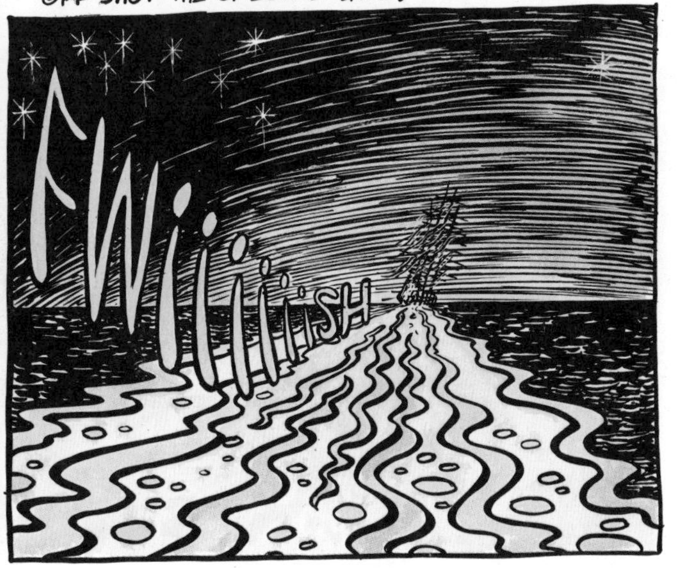
FWIIIIIISH

WE LISTENED AND LOOKED SIDEWAYS UP!
FEAR AT MY HEART, AS AT A CUP,
MY LIFE-BLOOD SEEMED TO SIP!
THE STARS WERE DIM, AND THICK THE NIGHT,
THE STEERSMAN'S FACE BY HIS LAMP GLEAMED WHITE;
FROM THE SAILS THE DEW DID DRIP—
TILL CLOMB ABOVE THE EASTERN BAR
THE HORNÉD MOON, WITH ONE BRIGHT STAR
WITHIN THE NETHER TIP....

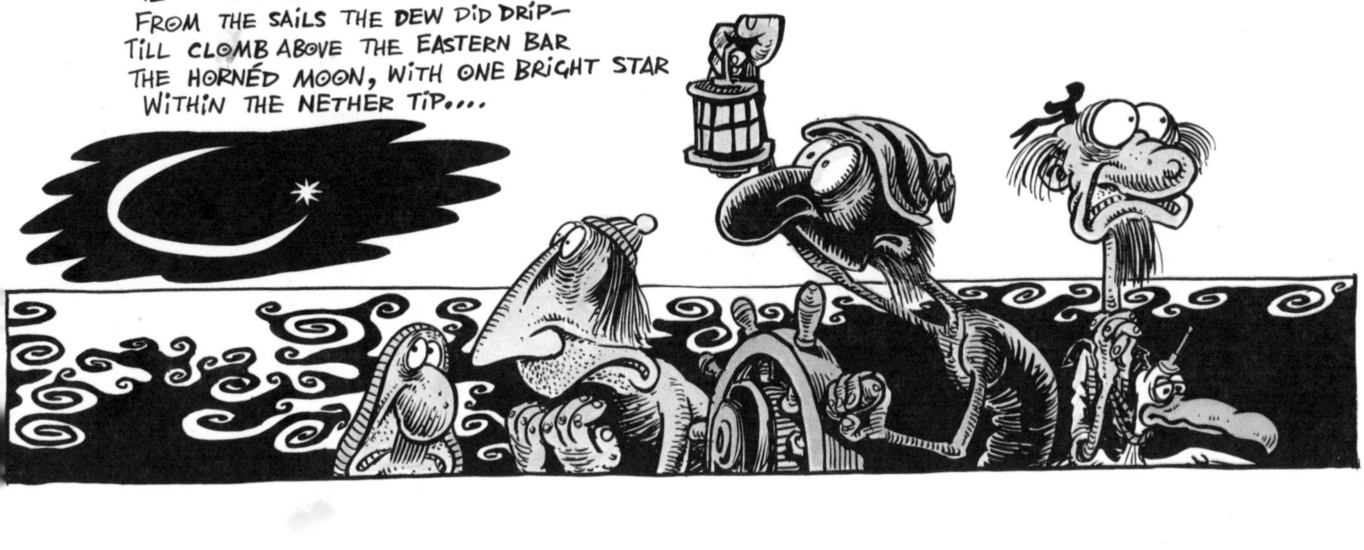

ONE AFTER ONE,
BY THE STAR-DOGGED MOON,
TOO QUICK FOR GROAN OR SIGH,
EACH TURNED HIS FACE
WITH GHASTLY PANG,
AND CURSED ME WITH HIS EYE!

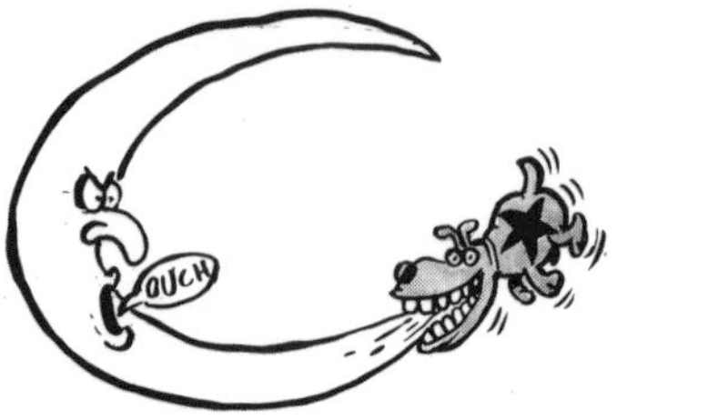
OUCH

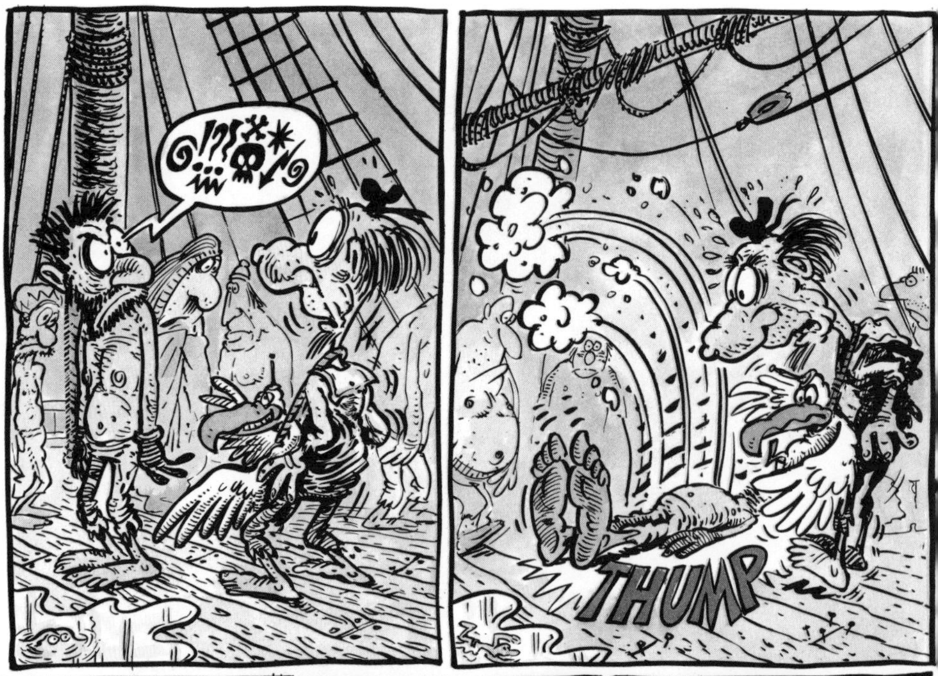
THUMP

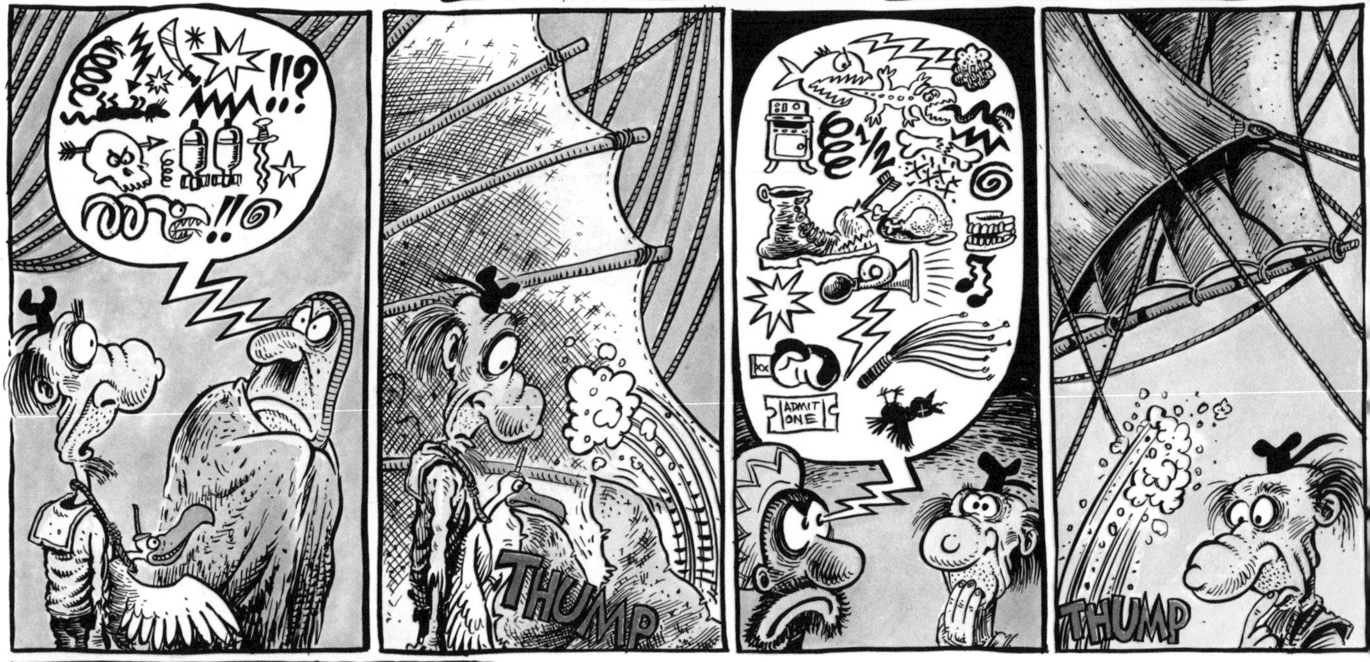
THUMP
ADMIT ONE
THUMP

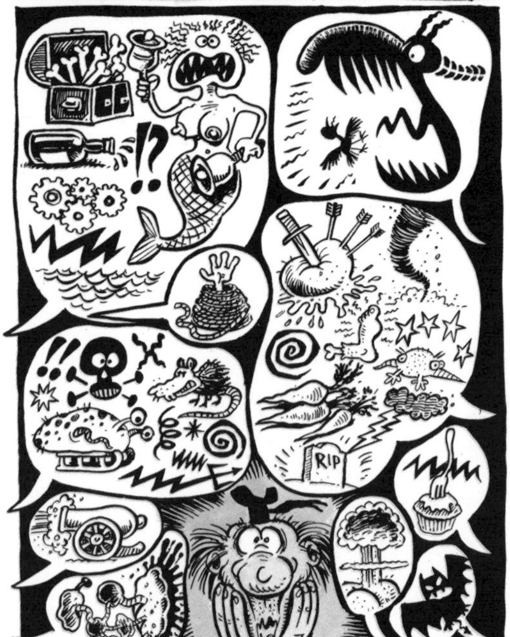
RIP

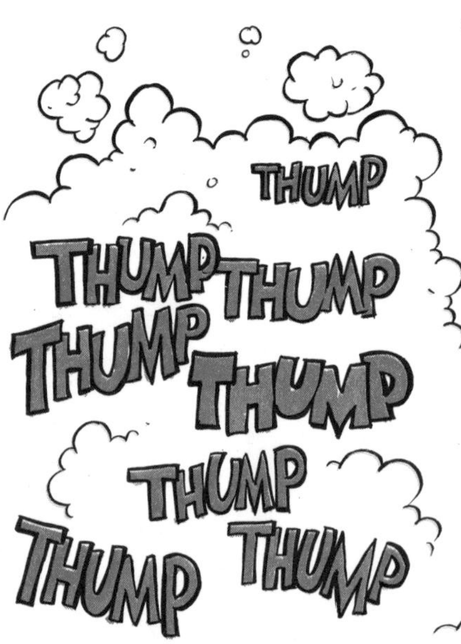
THUMP
THUMP THUMP
THUMP
THUMP
THUMP
THUMP THUMP

FOUR TIMES FIFTY LIVING MEN,
(AND I HEARD NOR SIGH NOR GROAN)
WITH HEAVY THUMP,
A LIFELESS LUMP,
THEY DROPPED DOWN
ONE BY ONE...

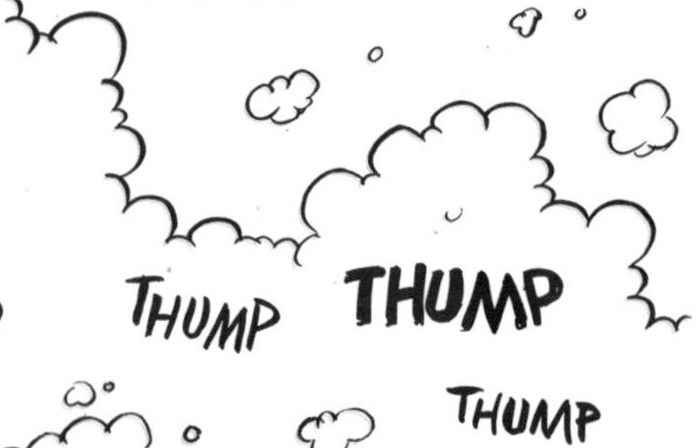
THUMP THUMP
THUMP

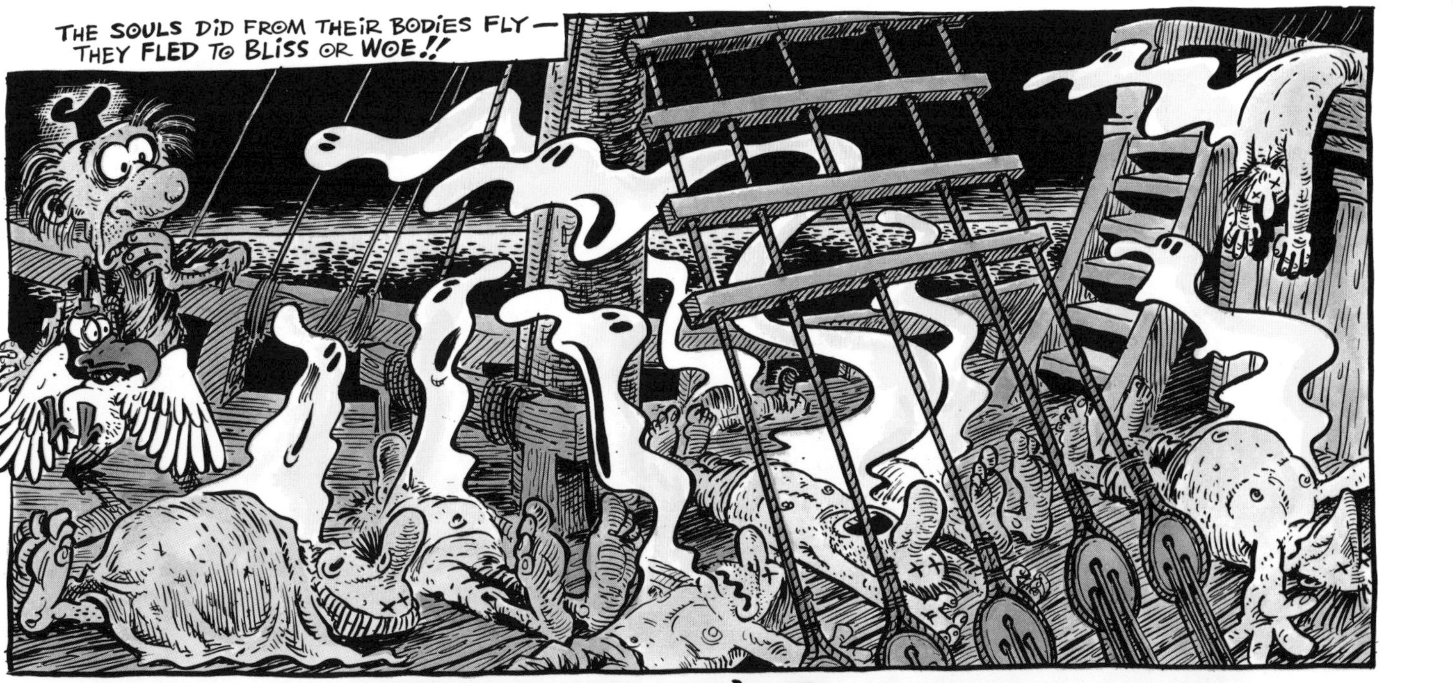
THE SOULS DID FROM THEIR BODIES FLY—
THEY FLED TO BLISS OR WOE!!

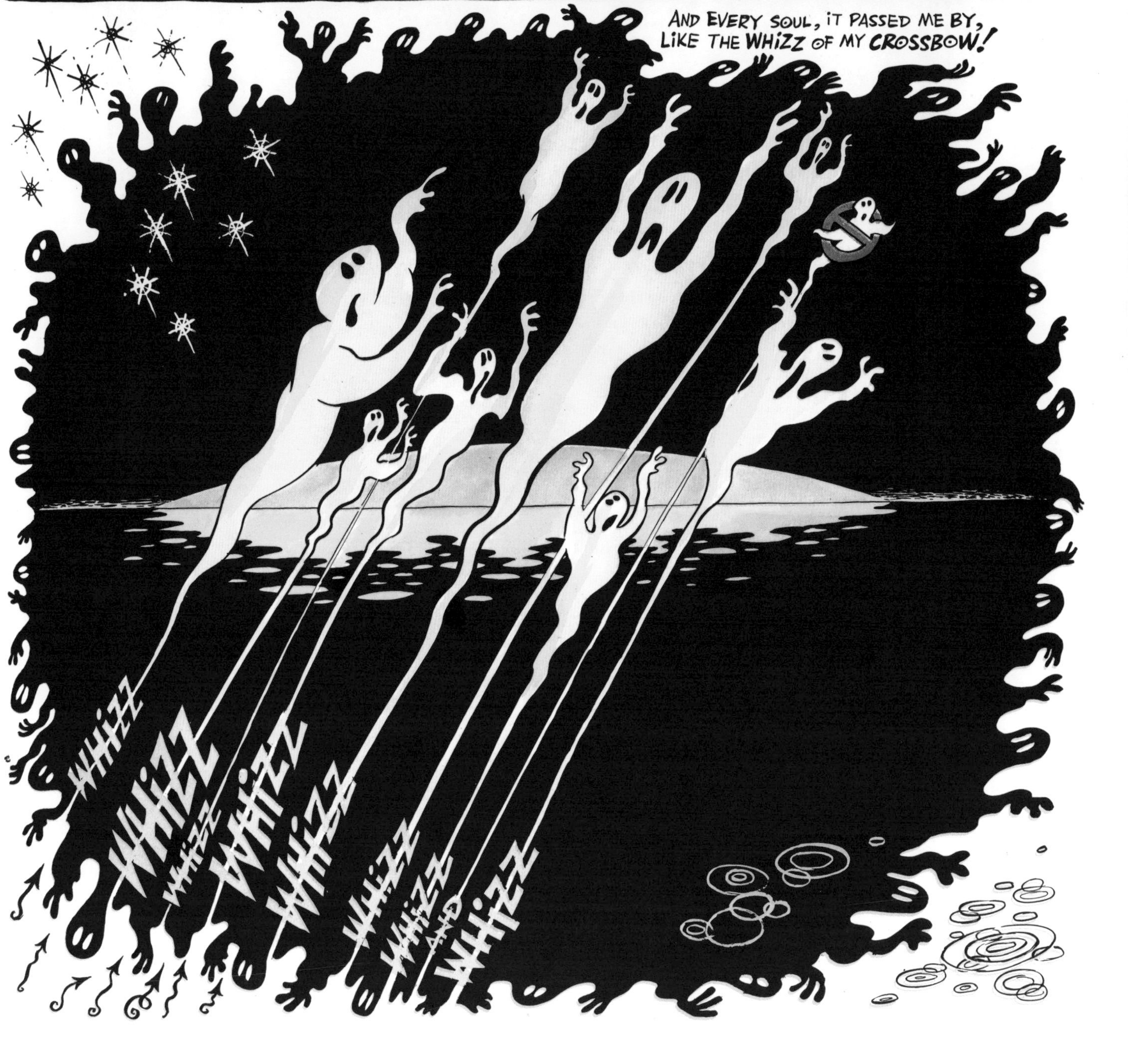
AND EVERY SOUL, IT PASSED ME BY,
LIKE THE WHIZZ OF MY CROSSBOW!
WHIZZ
WHIZZ
WHIZZ
WHIZZ
WHIZZ
WHIZZ
WHIZZ
AND
WHIZZ

part the fourth

*The Wedding-Guest feareth
that a Spirit is talking to him;*

*But the ancient Mariner assureth him of his bodily life,
and proceedeth to relate his horrible penance.*

He despiseth the creatures of the calm,

*And envieth that they should live,
and so many lie dead.*

But the curse liveth for him in the eye of the dead men.

*In his loneliness and fixedness he yearneth toward the
journeying Moon, and the stars that still sojourn, yet
still move onward; and every where the blue sky
belongs to them, and is their appointed rest, and their
native country and their own natural homes, which
they enter unannounced, as lords that are certainly
expected, and yet there is a silent joy at their arrival.*

*By the light of the Moon he beholdeth God's creatures
of the great calm.*

Their beauty and their happiness.

He blesseth them in his heart.

The spell begins to break.

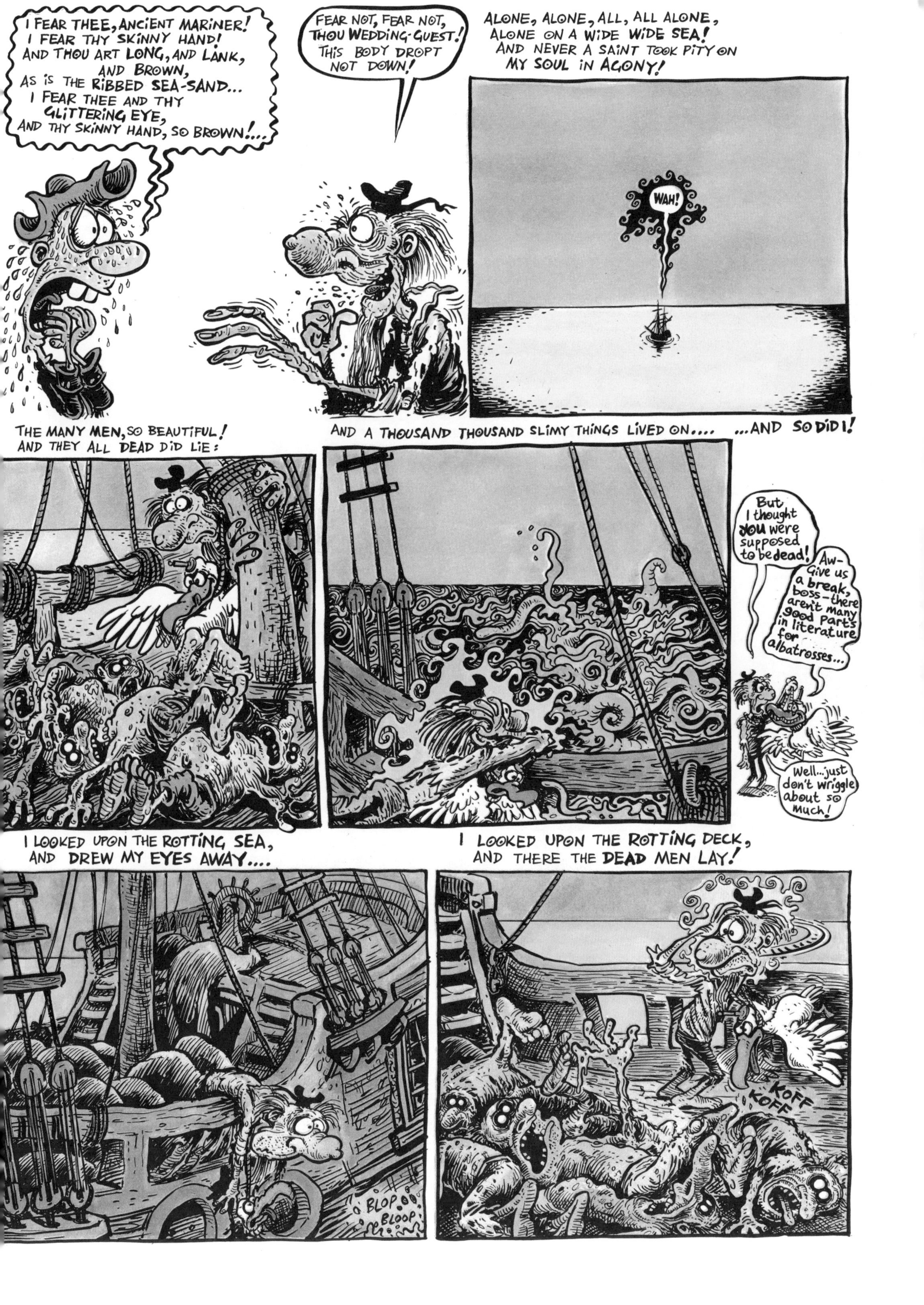
I FEAR THEE, ANCIENT MARINER! I FEAR THY SKINNY HAND! AND THOU ART LONG, AND LANK, AND BROWN, AS IS THE RIBBED SEA-SAND... I FEAR THEE AND THY GLITTERING EYE, AND THY SKINNY HAND, SO BROWN!...
FEAR NOT, FEAR NOT, THOU WEDDING-GUEST! THIS BODY DROPT NOT DOWN!
ALONE, ALONE, ALL, ALL ALONE, ALONE ON A WIDE WIDE SEA! AND NEVER A SAINT TOOK PITY ON MY SOUL IN AGONY!
WAH!
THE MANY MEN, SO BEAUTIFUL! AND THEY ALL DEAD DID LIE:
AND A THOUSAND THOUSAND SLIMY THINGS LIVED ON....
...AND SO DID I!
But I thought YOU were supposed to be dead!
Aw- Give us a break, boss-there aren't many good parts in literature for albatrosses...
Well... just don't wriggle about so much!
I LOOKED UPON THE ROTTING SEA, AND DREW MY EYES AWAY....
BLOP BLOOP
I LOOKED UPON THE ROTTING DECK, AND THERE THE DEAD MEN LAY!
KOFF KOFF

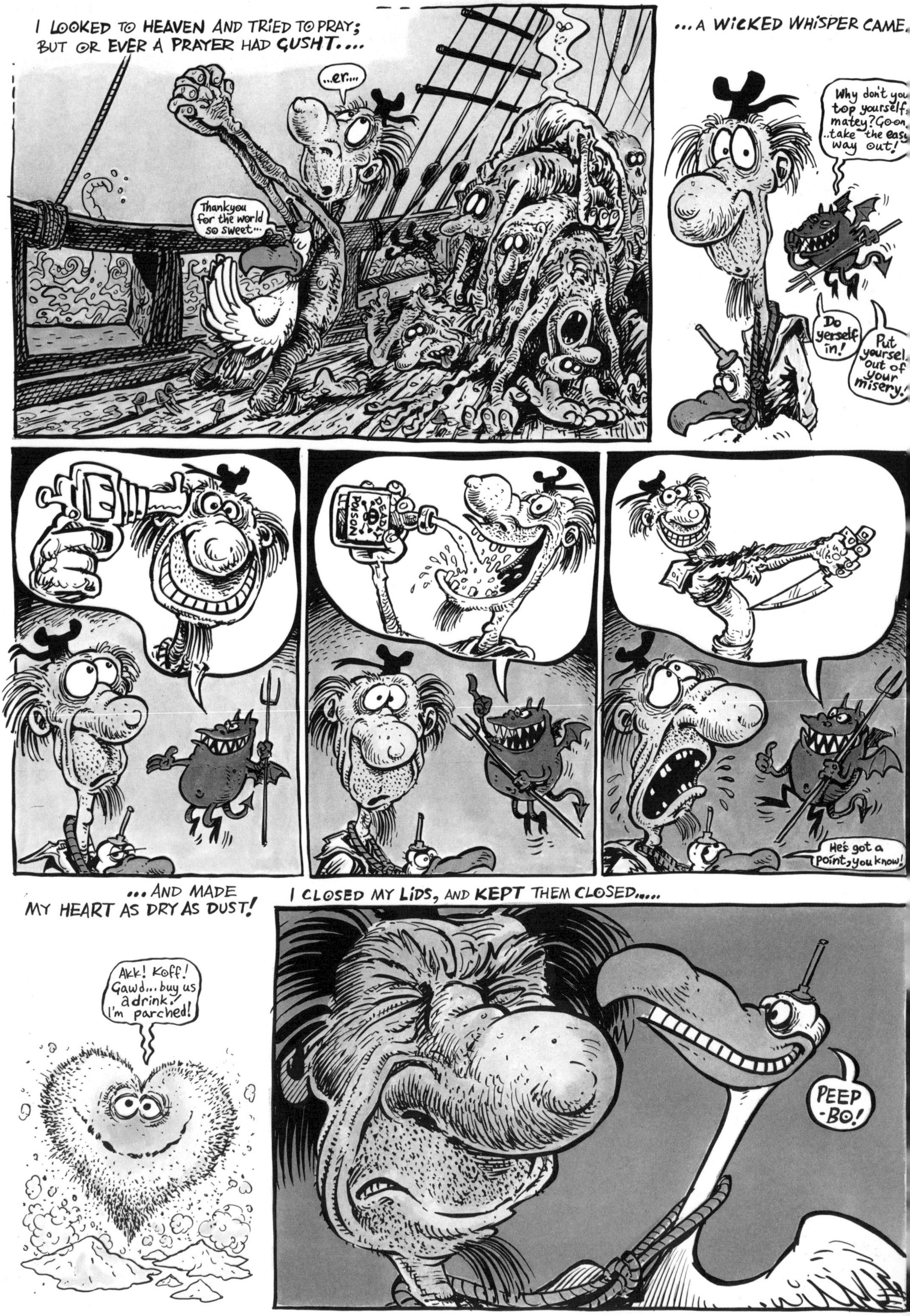
I LOOKED TO HEAVEN AND TRIED TO PRAY;
BUT OR EVER A PRAYER HAD GUSHT....
...er...
Thankyou for the world so sweet...
...A WICKED WHISPER CAME,
Why don't you top yourself, matey? Go on, ..take the eas way out!
Do yerself in!
Put yoursel out of your misery.
DEADLY POISON
He's got a point, you know!
...AND MADE MY HEART AS DRY AS DUST!
Akk! Koff! Gawd... buy us a drink! I'm parched!
I CLOSED MY LIDS, AND KEPT THEM CLOSED.....
PEEP-BO!

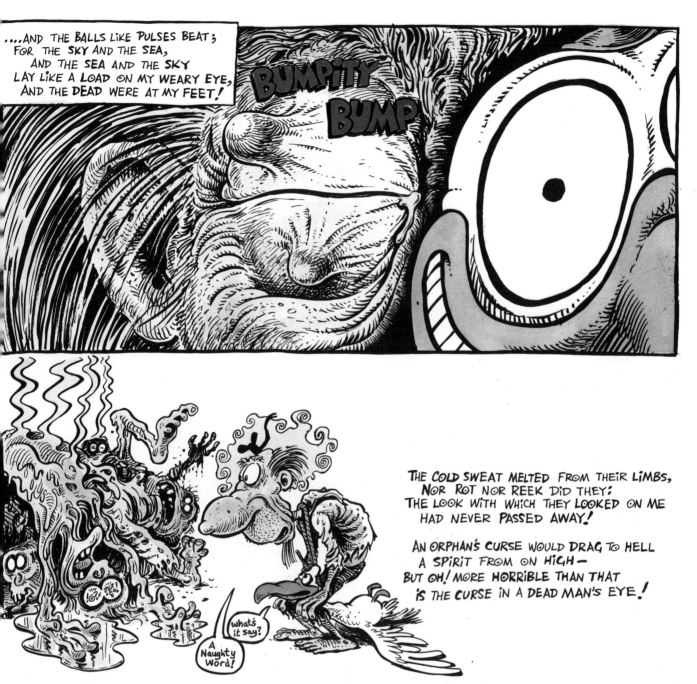

....AND THE BALLS LIKE PULSES BEAT;
FOR THE SKY AND THE SEA,
    AND THE SEA AND THE SKY
LAY LIKE A LOAD ON MY WEARY EYE,
AND THE DEAD WERE AT MY FEET!

BUMPITY BUMP

THE COLD SWEAT MELTED FROM THEIR LIMBS,
    NOR ROT NOR REEK DID THEY:
THE LOOK WITH WHICH THEY LOOKED ON ME
    HAD NEVER PASSED AWAY!

AN ORPHAN'S CURSE WOULD DRAG TO HELL
    A SPIRIT FROM ON HIGH —
BUT OH! MORE HORRIBLE THAN THAT
    IS THE CURSE IN A DEAD MAN'S EYE!

what's it say?

A Naughty Word!

SEVEN DAYS, SEVEN NIGHTS, I SAW THAT CURSE ...

...AND YET I COULD NOT DIE!

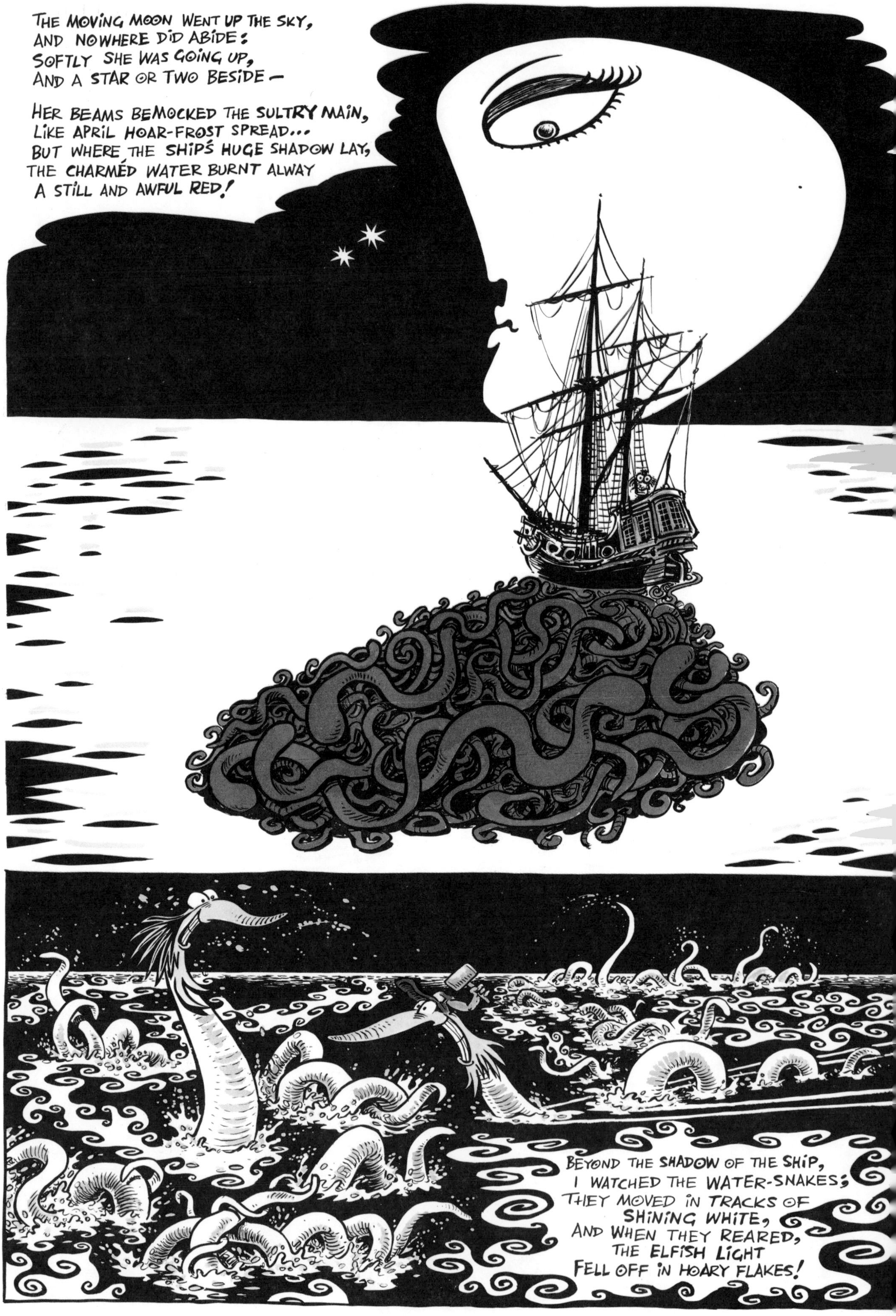
THE MOVING MOON WENT UP THE SKY,
AND NOWHERE DID ABIDE:
SOFTLY SHE WAS GOING UP,
AND A STAR OR TWO BESIDE—
HER BEAMS BEMOCKED THE SULTRY MAIN,
LIKE APRIL HOAR-FROST SPREAD...
BUT WHERE THE SHIP'S HUGE SHADOW LAY,
THE CHARMÉD WATER BURNT ALWAY
A STILL AND AWFUL RED!
BEYOND THE SHADOW OF THE SHIP,
I WATCHED THE WATER-SNAKES;
THEY MOVED IN TRACKS OF
SHINING WHITE,
AND WHEN THEY REARED,
THE ELFISH LIGHT
FELL OFF IN HOARY FLAKES!

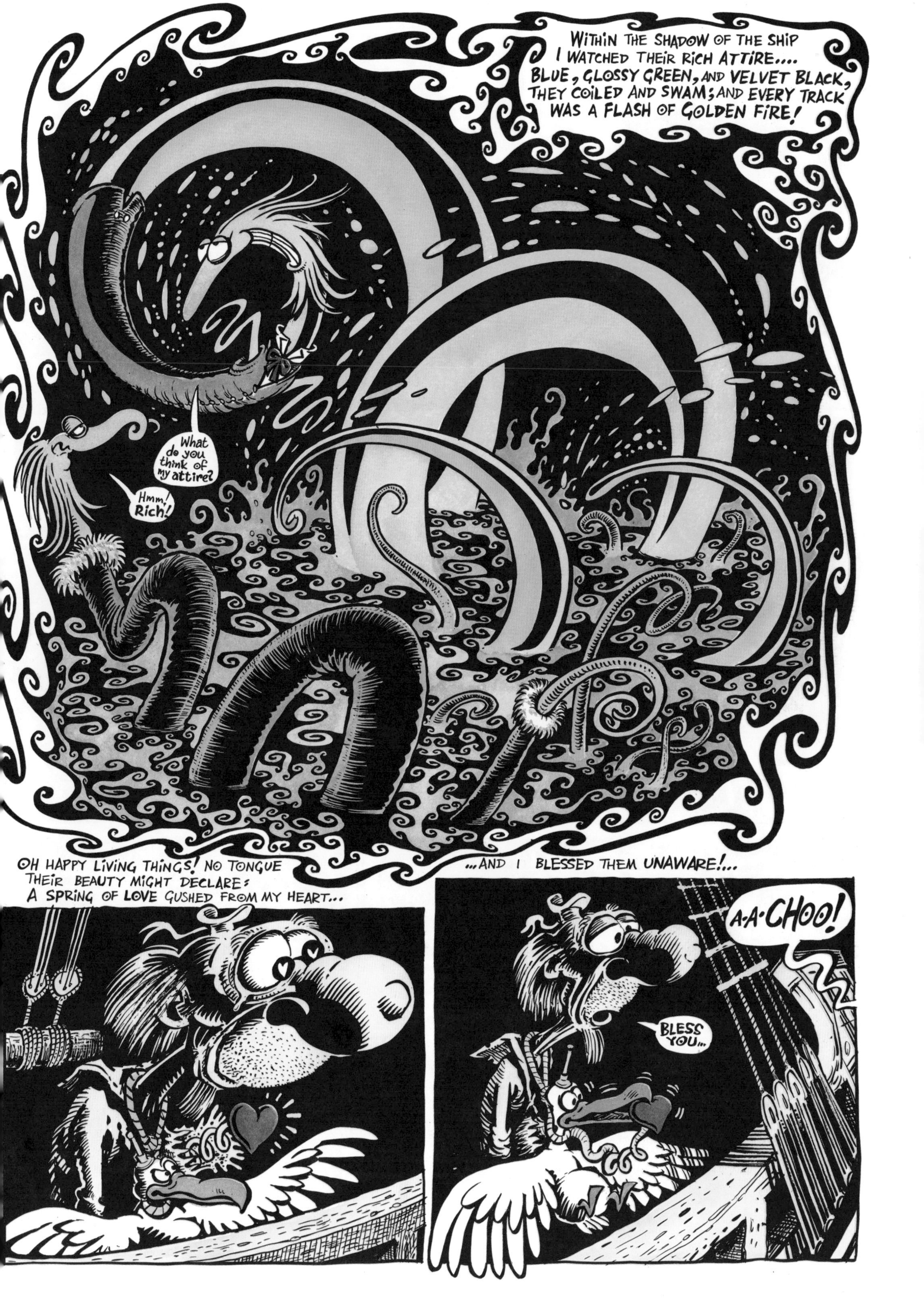
WITHIN THE SHADOW OF THE SHIP
I WATCHED THEIR RICH ATTIRE....
BLUE, GLOSSY GREEN, AND VELVET BLACK,
THEY COILED AND SWAM; AND EVERY TRACK
WAS A FLASH OF GOLDEN FIRE!
What do you think of my attire?
Hmm! Rich!
OH HAPPY LIVING THINGS! NO TONGUE
THEIR BEAUTY MIGHT DECLARE:
A SPRING OF LOVE GUSHED FROM MY HEART...
...AND I BLESSED THEM UNAWARE!...
A-A-CHOO!
BLESS YOU...

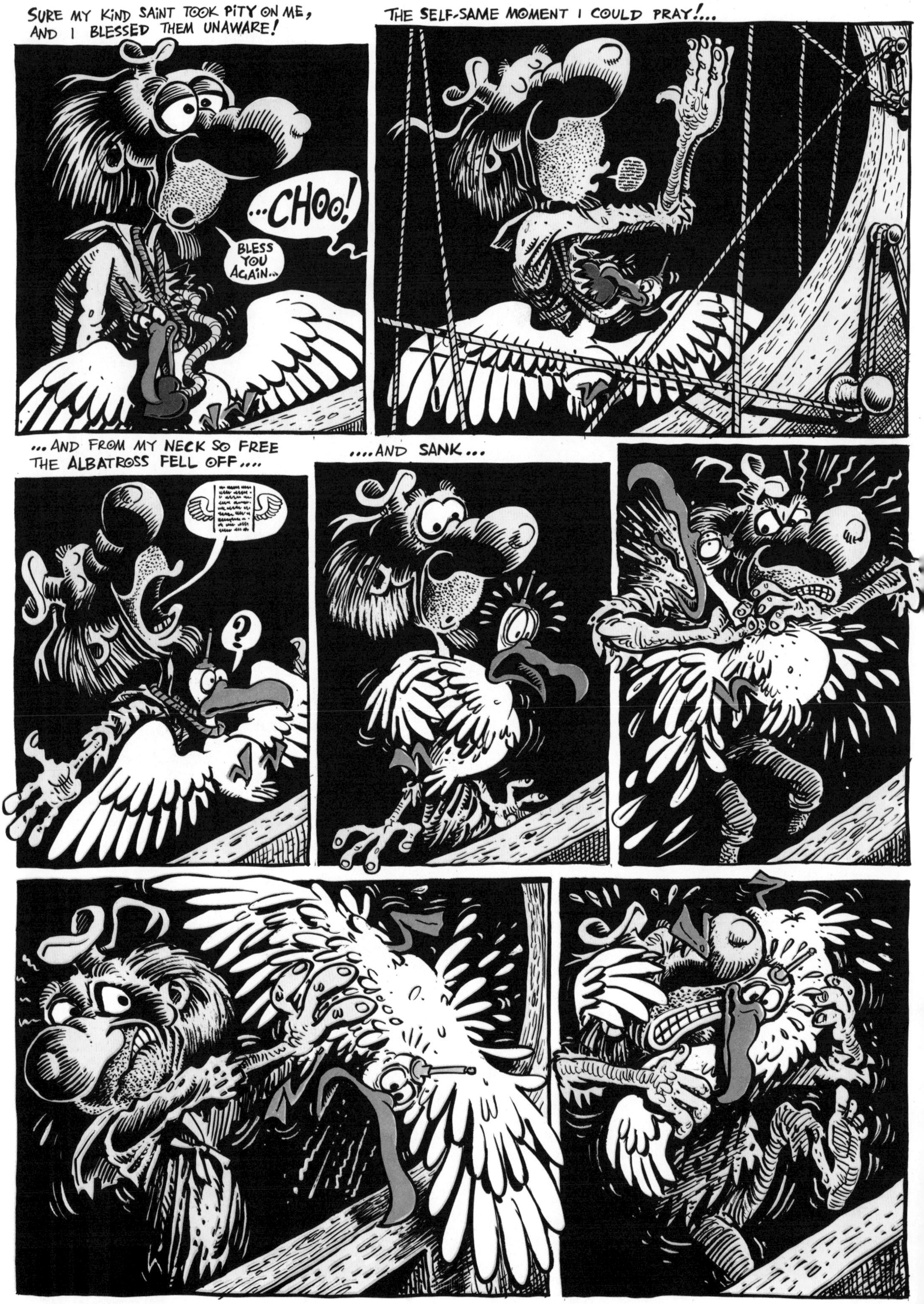
SURE MY KIND SAINT TOOK PITY ON ME, AND I BLESSED THEM UNAWARE!
...CHOO!
BLESS YOU AGAIN...
THE SELF-SAME MOMENT I COULD PRAY!...
...AND FROM MY NECK SO FREE THE ALBATROSS FELL OFF....
?
....AND SANK...

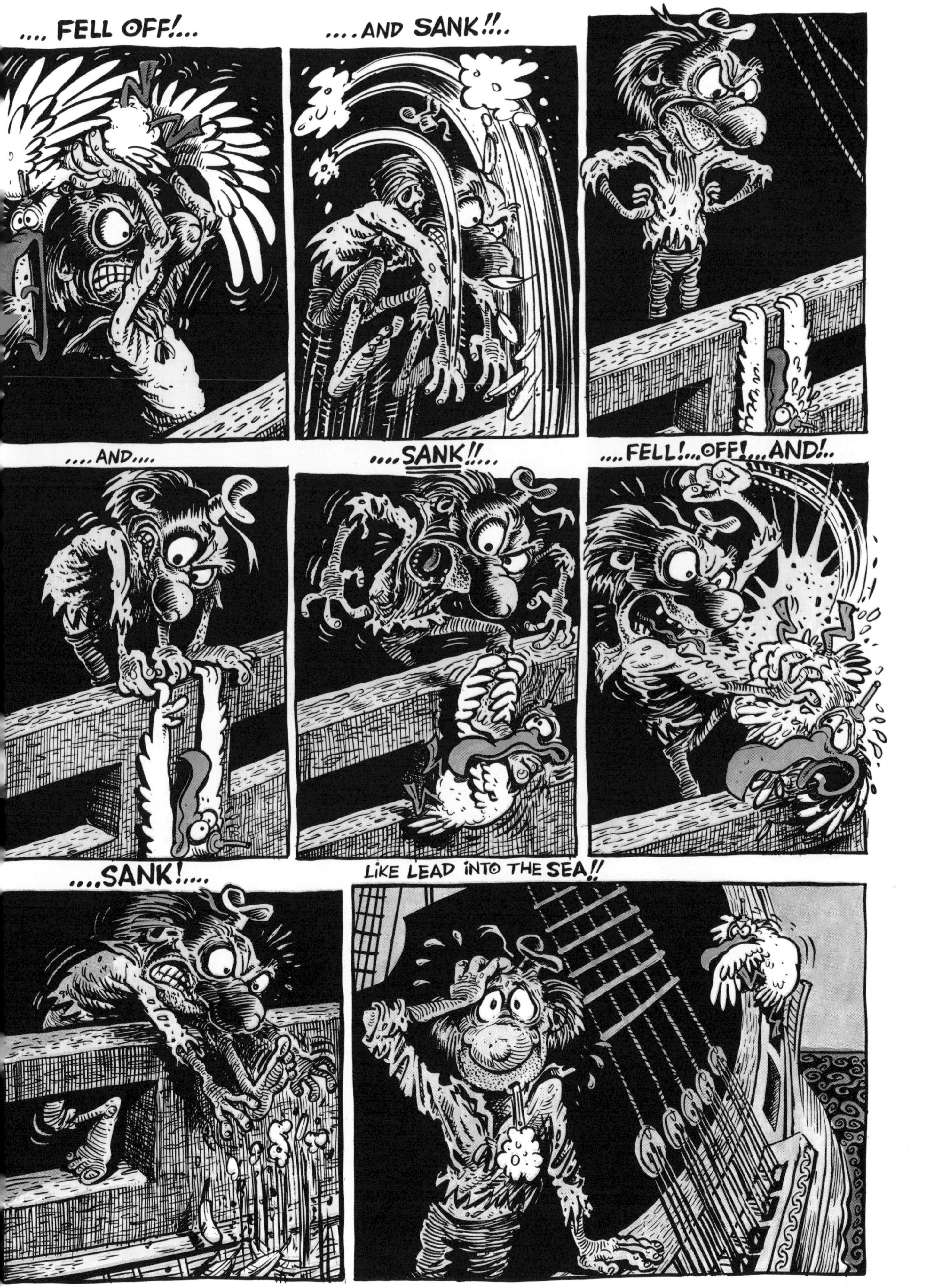
.... FELL OFF!...
.... AND SANK!!..
....AND....
....SANK!!...
....FELL!...OFF!...AND!..
....SANK!....
LIKE LEAD INTO THE SEA!!

part the fifth

By grace of the Holy Mother, the ancient Mariner is refreshed with rain.

He heareth sounds and seeth strange sights and commotions in the sky and the element.

The bodies of the ship's crew are inspired, and the ship moves on;

But not by the souls of the men, nor by demons of earth or middle air, but by a blessed troop of angelic spirits, sent down by the invocation of the guardian saint.

The lonesome Spirit from the south pole carries on the ship as far as the line, in obedience to the angelic troop, but still requireth vengeance.

The Polar Spirit's fellow-demons, the invisible inhabitants of the element, take part in his wrong; and two of them relate, one to the other, that penance long and heavy for the ancient Mariner hath been accorded to the Polar Spirit, who returneth southward.

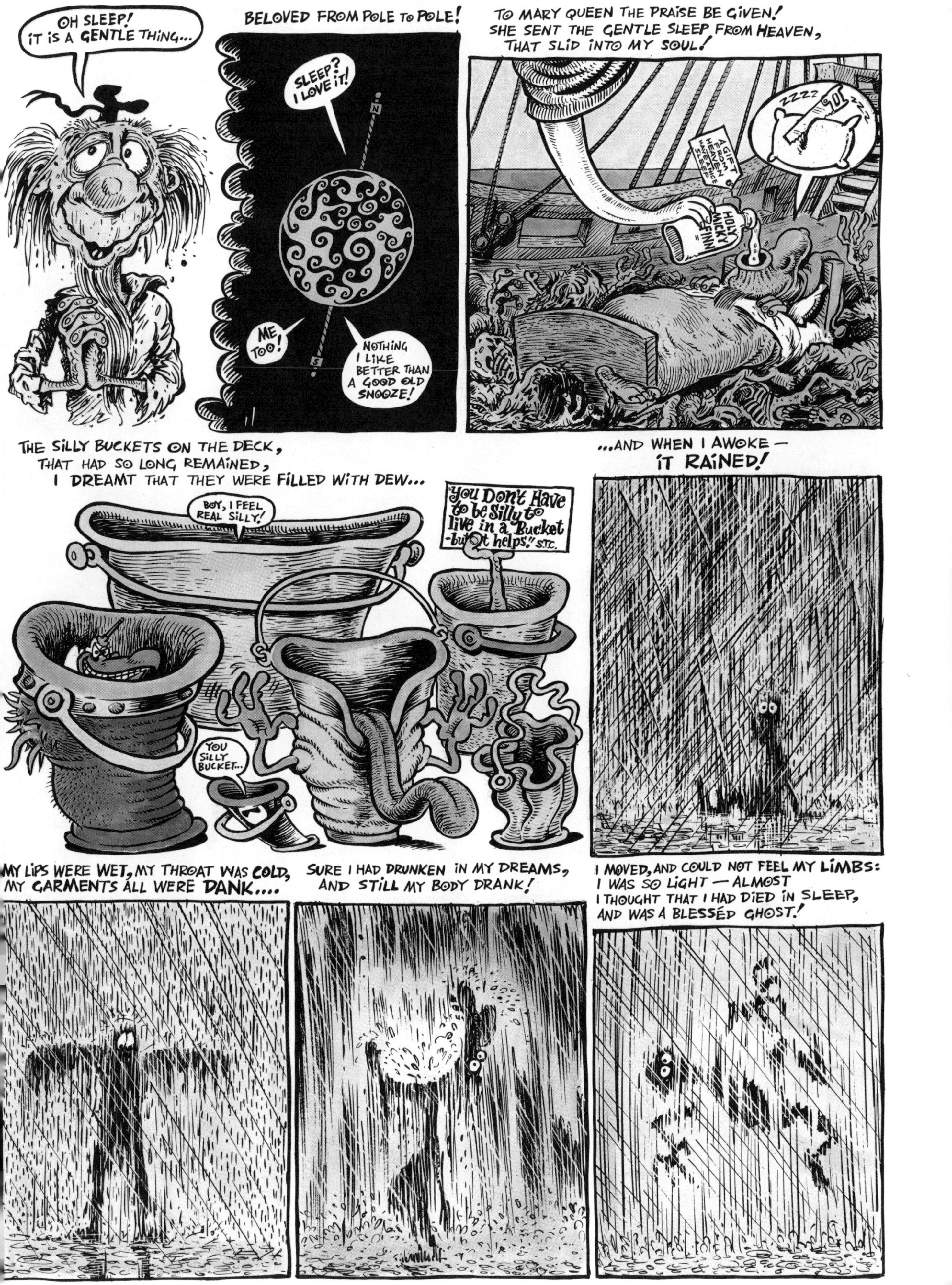
OH SLEEP! IT IS A GENTLE THING...
BELOVED FROM POLE TO POLE!
SLEEP? I LOVE IT!
ME TOO!
NOTHING I LIKE BETTER THAN A GOOD OLD SNOOZE!
TO MARY QUEEN THE PRAISE BE GIVEN!
SHE SENT THE GENTLE SLEEP FROM HEAVEN,
THAT SLID INTO MY SOUL!
ZZZZ
A GIFT FROM HEAVEN
HOLY MICKY FINN
THE SILLY BUCKETS ON THE DECK,
THAT HAD SO LONG REMAINED,
I DREAMT THAT THEY WERE FILLED WITH DEW...
BOY, I FEEL REAL SILLY!
"You Don't Have to be Silly to live in a Bucket - but it helps!" S.T.C.
YOU SILLY BUCKET...
...AND WHEN I AWOKE —
IT RAINED!
MY LIPS WERE WET, MY THROAT WAS COLD,
MY GARMENTS ALL WERE DANK....
SURE I HAD DRUNKEN IN MY DREAMS,
AND STILL MY BODY DRANK!
I MOVED, AND COULD NOT FEEL MY LIMBS:
I WAS SO LIGHT — ALMOST
I THOUGHT THAT I HAD DIED IN SLEEP,
AND WAS A BLESSÉD GHOST!

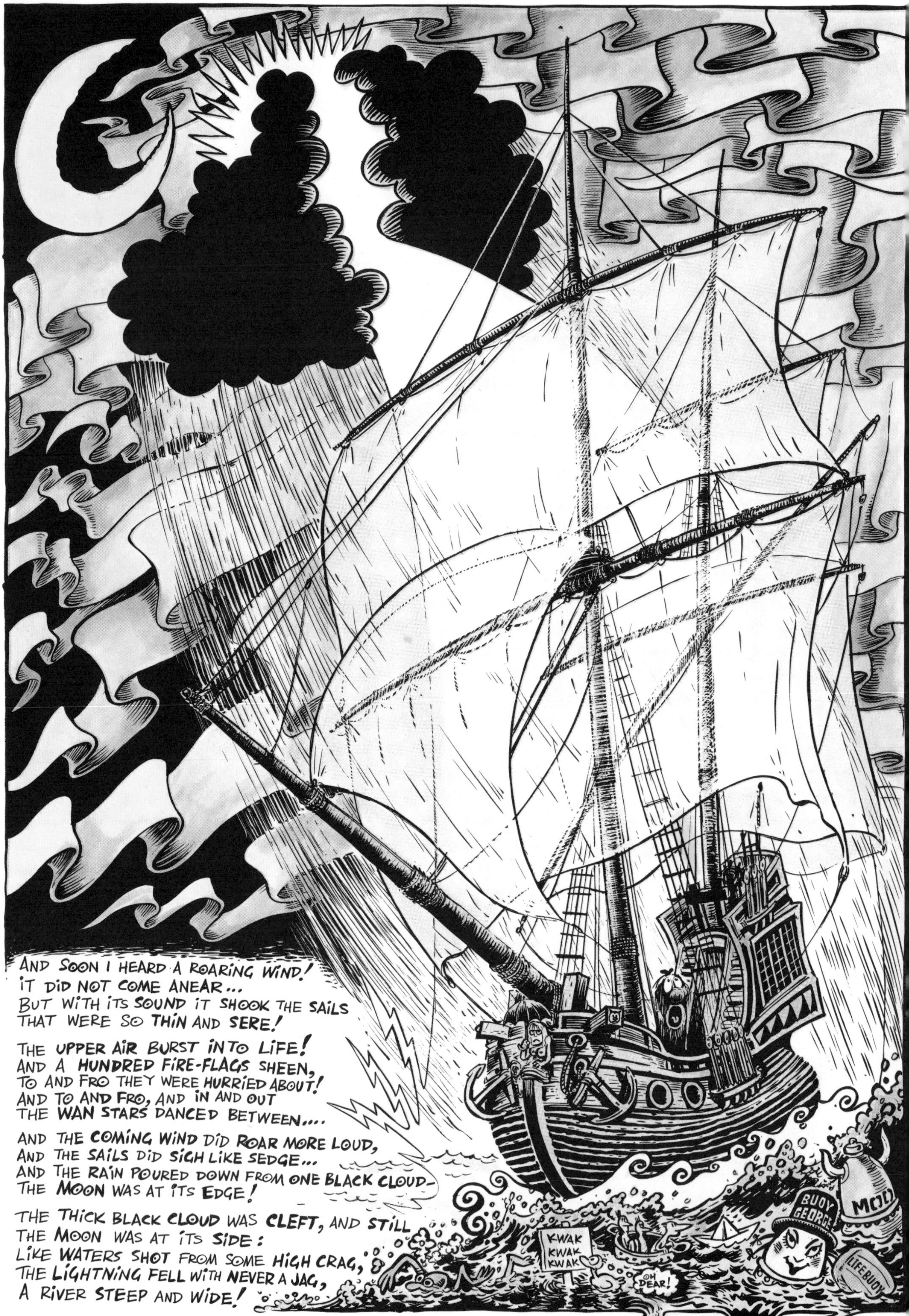
AND SOON I HEARD A ROARING WIND! IT DID NOT COME ANEAR... BUT WITH ITS SOUND IT SHOOK THE SAILS THAT WERE SO THIN AND SERE!
THE UPPER AIR BURST INTO LIFE! AND A HUNDRED FIRE-FLAGS SHEEN, TO AND FRO THEY WERE HURRIED ABOUT! AND TO AND FRO, AND IN AND OUT THE WAN STARS DANCED BETWEEN....
AND THE COMING WIND DID ROAR MORE LOUD, AND THE SAILS DID SIGH LIKE SEDGE... AND THE RAIN POURED DOWN FROM ONE BLACK CLOUD- THE MOON WAS AT ITS EDGE!
THE THICK BLACK CLOUD WAS CLEFT, AND STILL THE MOON WAS AT ITS SIDE: LIKE WATERS SHOT FROM SOME HIGH CRAG, THE LIGHTNING FELL WITH NEVER A JAG, A RIVER STEEP AND WIDE!
KWAK KWAK KWAK
OH DEAR!
BUOY GEORGE
LIFEBUOY

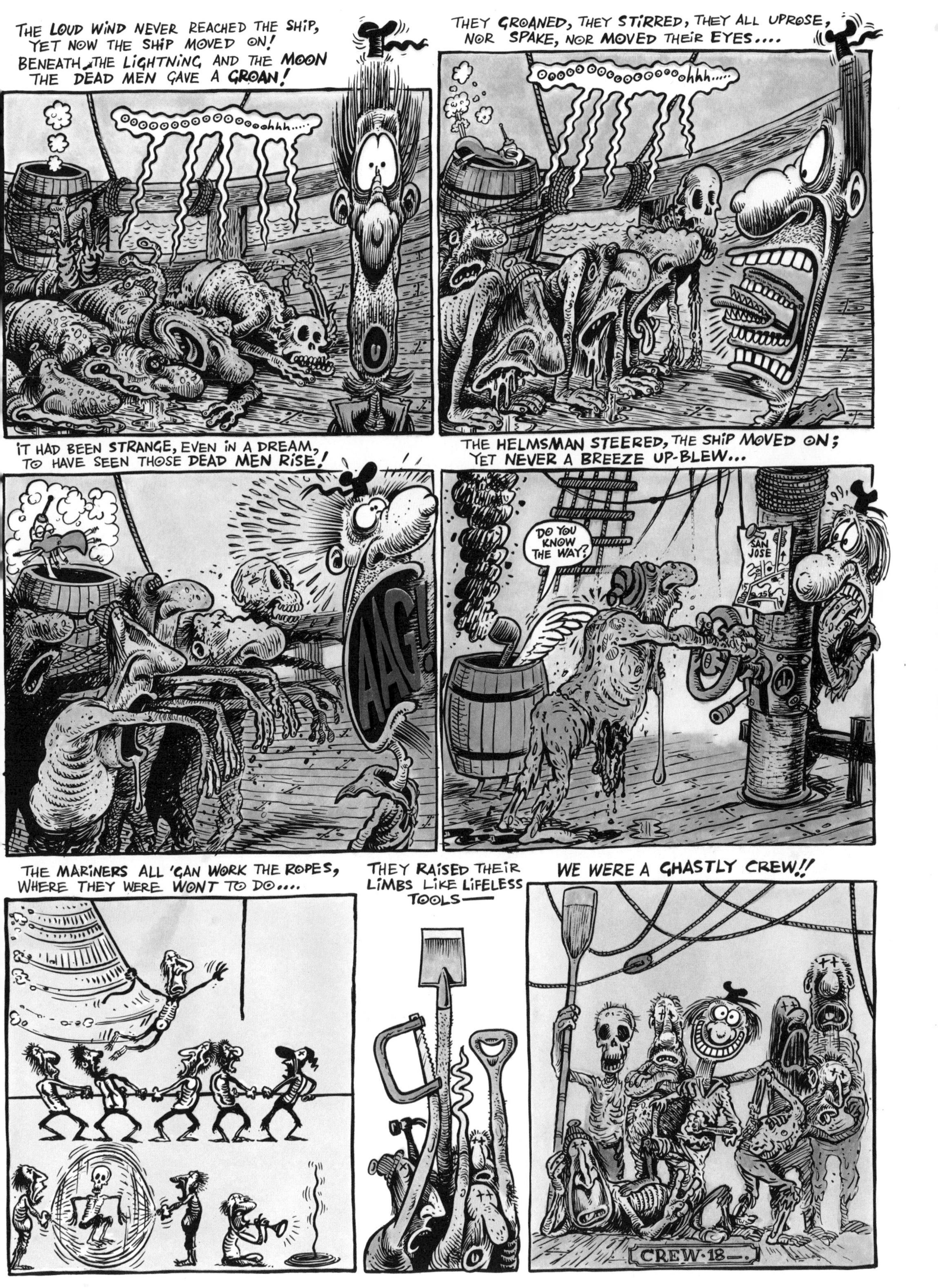

THE LOUD WIND NEVER REACHED THE SHIP, YET NOW THE SHIP MOVED ON! BENEATH THE LIGHTNING AND THE MOON THE DEAD MEN GAVE A GROAN!
Oooooooooooooooohhh.....
THEY GROANED, THEY STIRRED, THEY ALL UPROSE, NOR SPAKE, NOR MOVED THEIR EYES....
Ooooo oooooooooohhh.....
IT HAD BEEN STRANGE, EVEN IN A DREAM, TO HAVE SEEN THOSE DEAD MEN RISE!
AAG!
THE HELMSMAN STEERED, THE SHIP MOVED ON; YET NEVER A BREEZE UP-BLEW...
DO YOU KNOW THE WAY?
SAN JOSE
THE MARINERS ALL 'GAN WORK THE ROPES, WHERE THEY WERE WONT TO DO....
THEY RAISED THEIR LIMBS LIKE LIFELESS TOOLS—
WE WERE A GHASTLY CREW!!
CREW·18—.

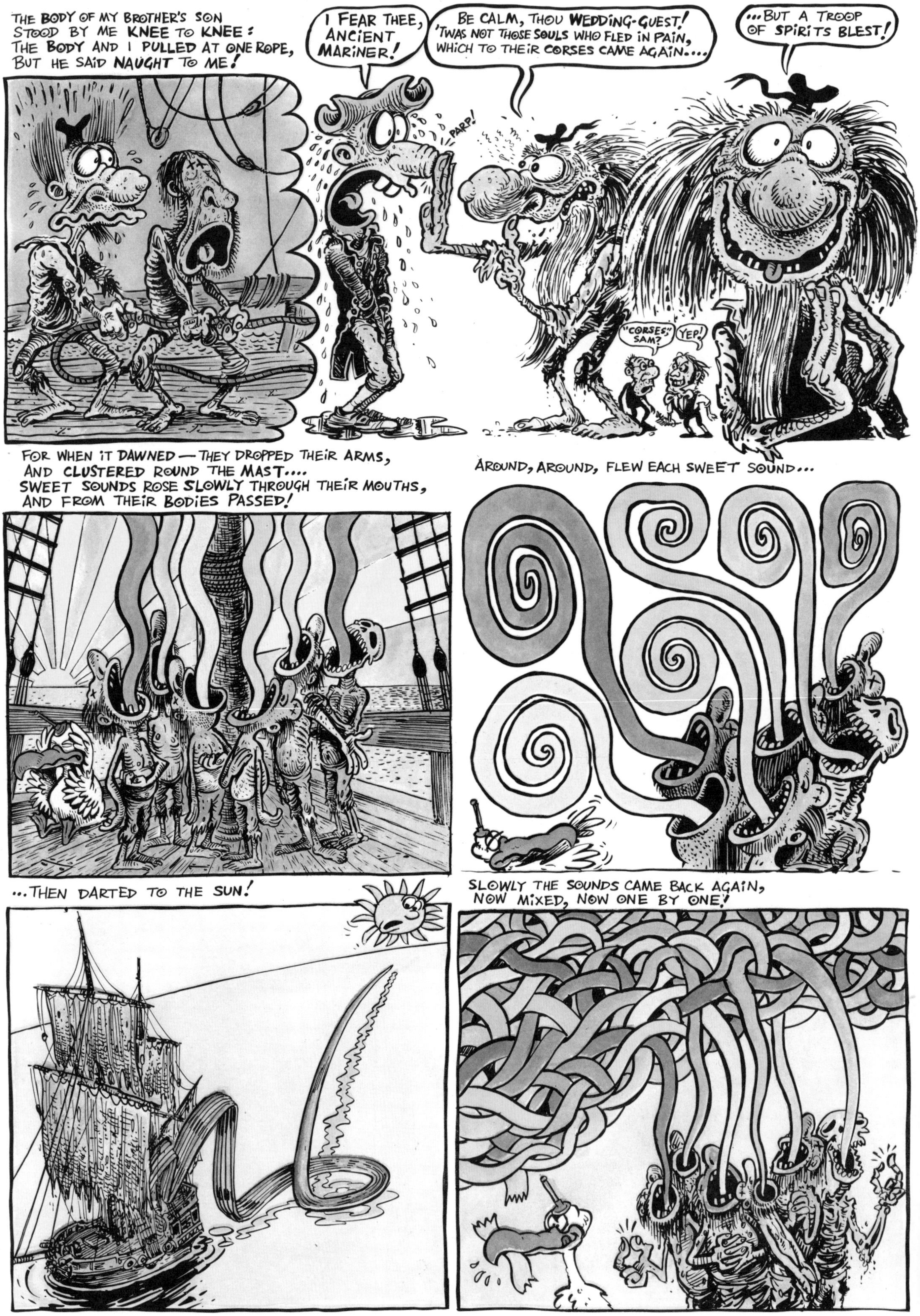

THE BODY OF MY BROTHER'S SON
STOOD BY ME KNEE TO KNEE:
THE BODY AND I PULLED AT ONE ROPE,
BUT HE SAID NAUGHT TO ME!
I FEAR THEE, ANCIENT MARINER!
PARP!
BE CALM, THOU WEDDING-GUEST! 'TWAS NOT THOSE SOULS WHO FLED IN PAIN, WHICH TO THEIR CORSES CAME AGAIN....
...BUT A TROOP OF SPIRITS BLEST!
"CORSES," SAM?
YEP!
FOR WHEN IT DAWNED — THEY DROPPED THEIR ARMS,
AND CLUSTERED ROUND THE MAST....
SWEET SOUNDS ROSE SLOWLY THROUGH THEIR MOUTHS,
AND FROM THEIR BODIES PASSED!
AROUND, AROUND, FLEW EACH SWEET SOUND...
...THEN DARTED TO THE SUN!
SLOWLY THE SOUNDS CAME BACK AGAIN,
NOW MIXED, NOW ONE BY ONE!

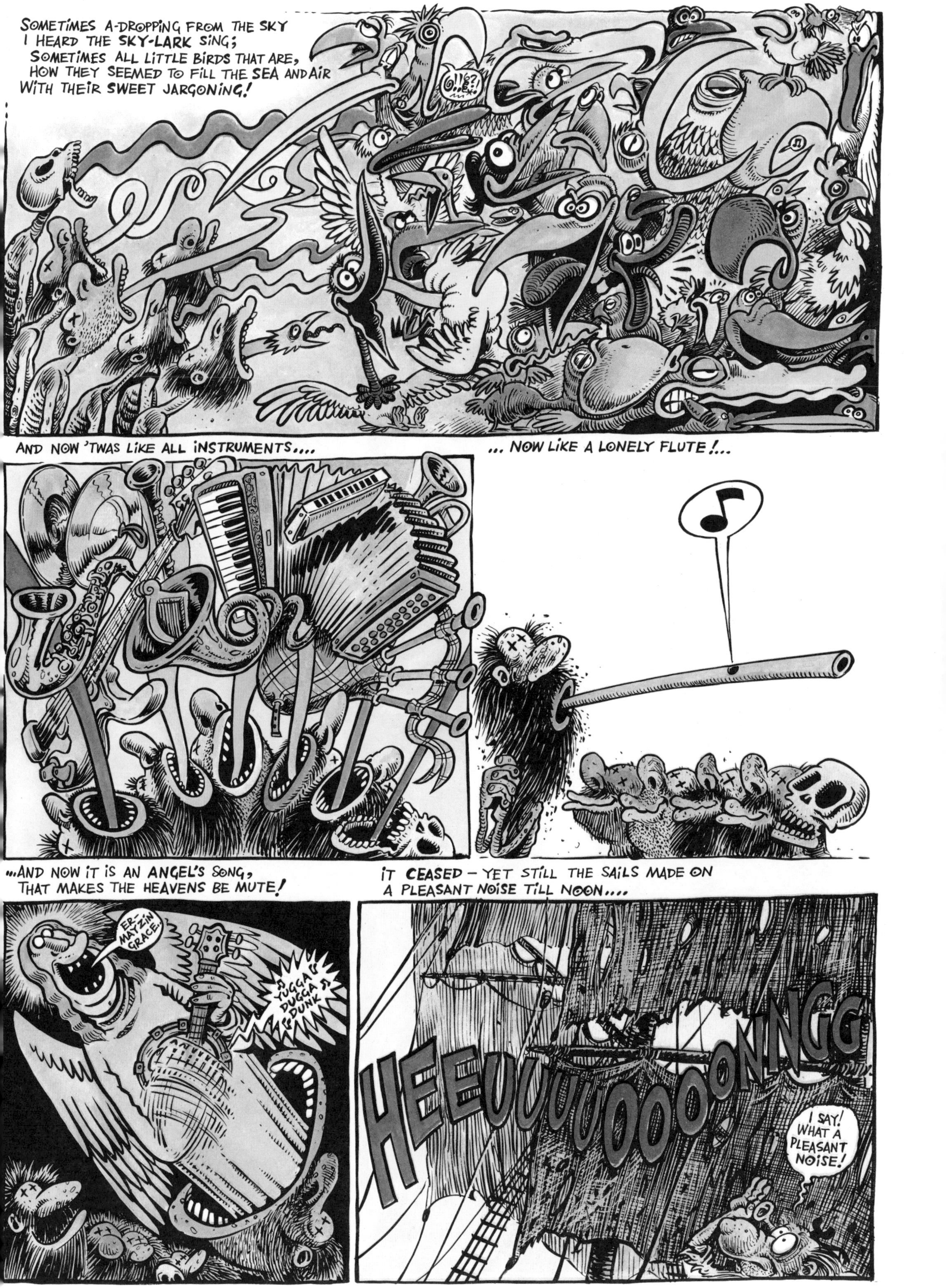
SOMETIMES A-DROPPING FROM THE SKY
I HEARD THE SKY-LARK SING;
SOMETIMES ALL LITTLE BIRDS THAT ARE,
HOW THEY SEEMED TO FILL THE SEA AND AIR
WITH THEIR SWEET JARGONING!
AND NOW 'TWAS LIKE ALL INSTRUMENTS....
... NOW LIKE A LONELY FLUTE!...
...AND NOW IT IS AN ANGEL'S SONG,
THAT MAKES THE HEAVENS BE MUTE!
ER-MAYZIN GRACE!
YUGGA DUGGA DUNK
IT CEASED — YET STILL THE SAILS MADE ON
A PLEASANT NOISE TILL NOON....
HEEUUUUUOOOOONNGG
I SAY! WHAT A PLEASANT NOISE!

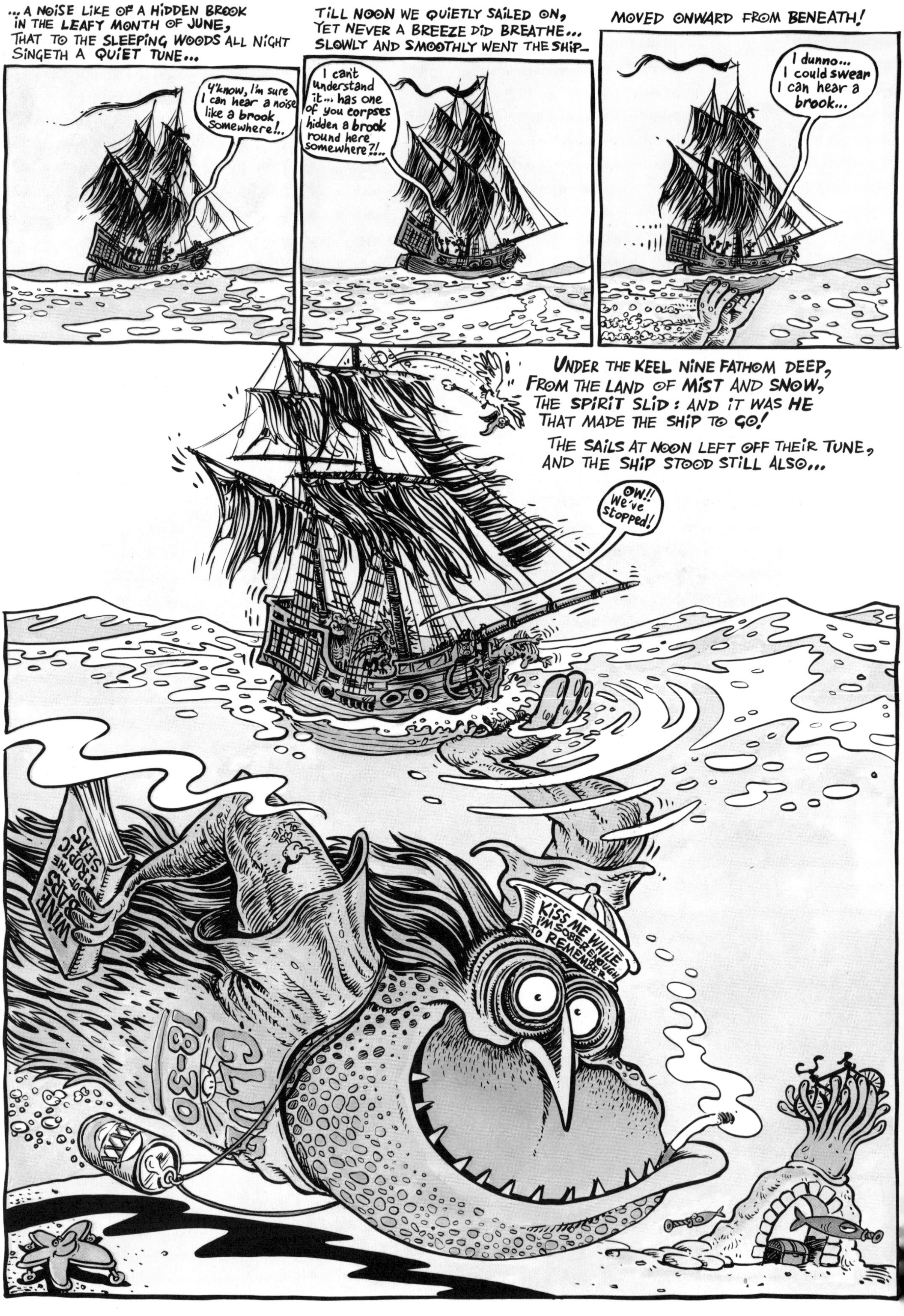
...A NOISE LIKE OF A HIDDEN BROOK
IN THE LEAFY MONTH OF JUNE,
THAT TO THE SLEEPING WOODS ALL NIGHT
SINGETH A QUIET TUNE...
Y'know, I'm sure I can hear a noise like a brook somewhere!..
TILL NOON WE QUIETLY SAILED ON,
YET NEVER A BREEZE DID BREATHE...
SLOWLY AND SMOOTHLY WENT THE SHIP-
I can't understand it... has one of you corpses hidden a brook round here somewhere?!..
MOVED ONWARD FROM BENEATH!
I dunno... I could swear I can hear a brook...
UNDER THE KEEL NINE FATHOM DEEP,
FROM THE LAND OF MIST AND SNOW,
THE SPIRIT SLID: AND IT WAS HE
THAT MADE THE SHIP TO GO!
THE SAILS AT NOON LEFT OFF THEIR TUNE,
AND THE SHIP STOOD STILL ALSO...
OW!! We've stopped!
WINE BARS OF THE TROPIC SEAS
KISS ME WHILE I'M SOBER ENOUGH TO REMEMBER
CLUB 18-30

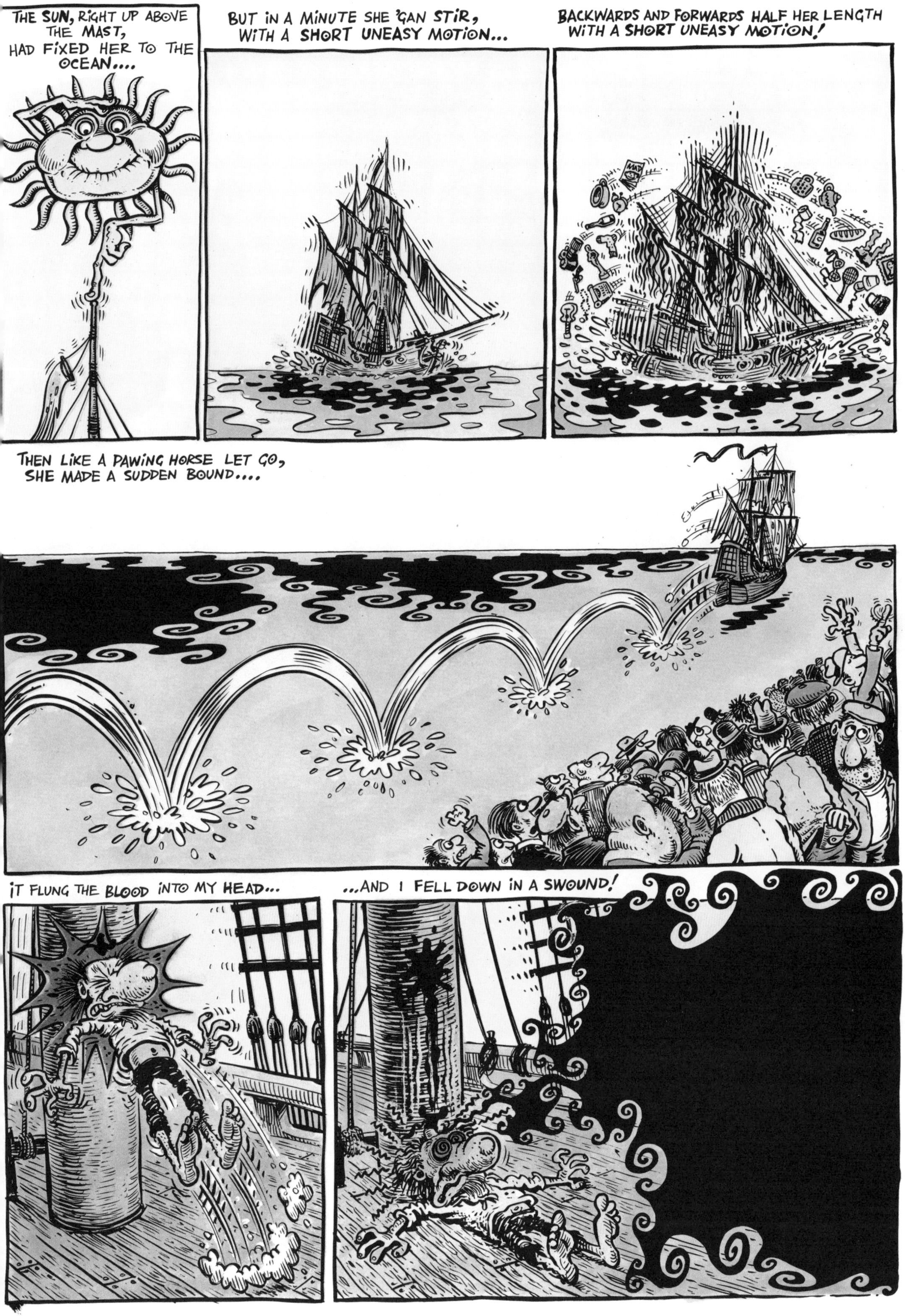
THE SUN, RIGHT UP ABOVE THE MAST, HAD FIXED HER TO THE OCEAN....
BUT IN A MINUTE SHE 'GAN STIR, WITH A SHORT UNEASY MOTION...
BACKWARDS AND FORWARDS HALF HER LENGTH WITH A SHORT UNEASY MOTION!
THEN LIKE A PAWING HORSE LET GO, SHE MADE A SUDDEN BOUND....
IT FLUNG THE BLOOD INTO MY HEAD...
...AND I FELL DOWN IN A SWOUND!

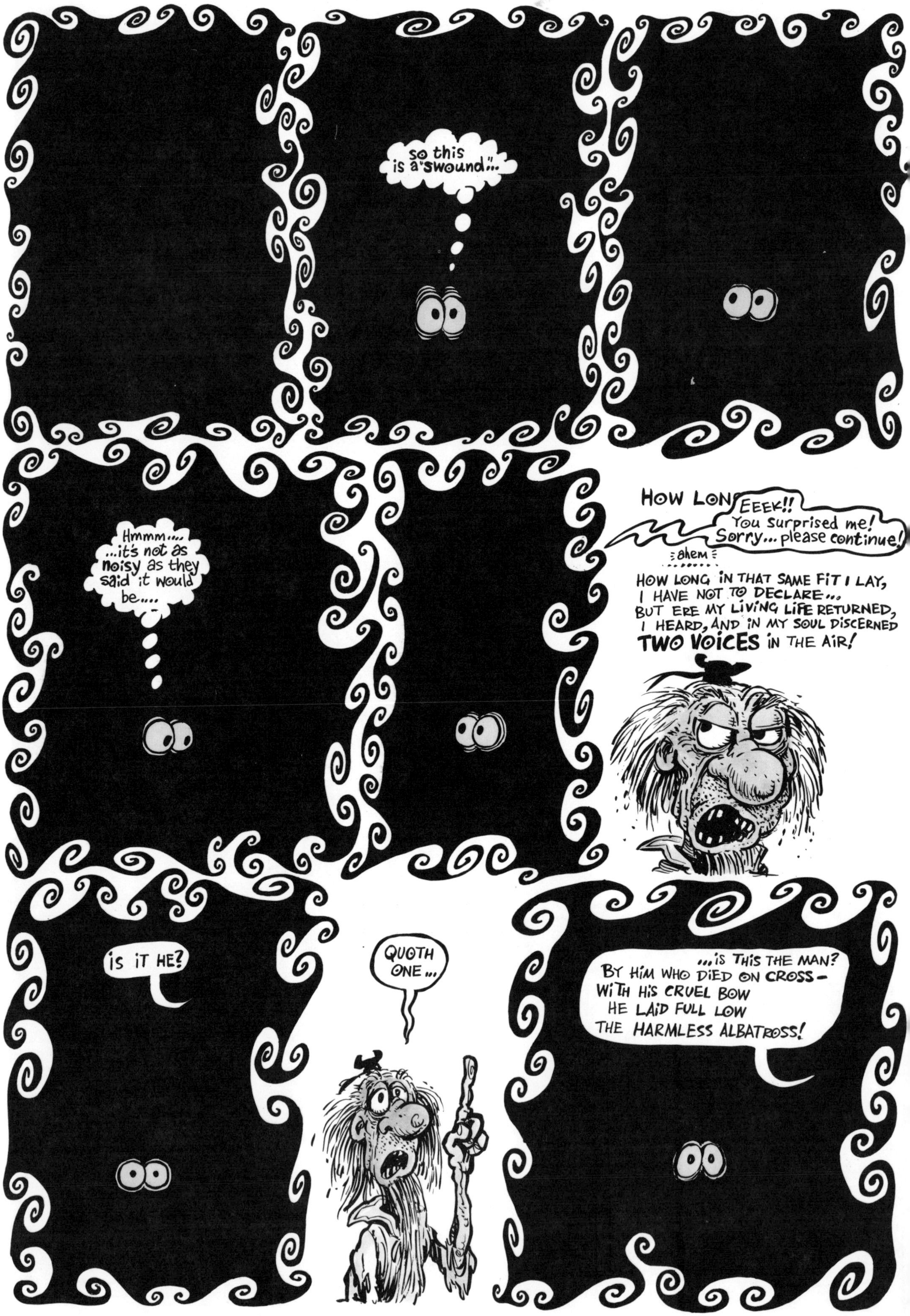
so this is a "swound"...
Hmmm.... ...it's not as noisy as they said it would be....
HOW LONG
EEEK!! You surprised me! Sorry... please continue!
ahem
HOW LONG IN THAT SAME FIT I LAY, I HAVE NOT TO DECLARE... BUT ERE MY LIVING LIFE RETURNED, I HEARD, AND IN MY SOUL DISCERNED TWO VOICES IN THE AIR!
is it HE?
QUOTH ONE...
...is THIS THE MAN? BY HIM WHO DIED ON CROSS- WITH HIS CRUEL BOW HE LAID FULL LOW THE HARMLESS ALBATROSS!

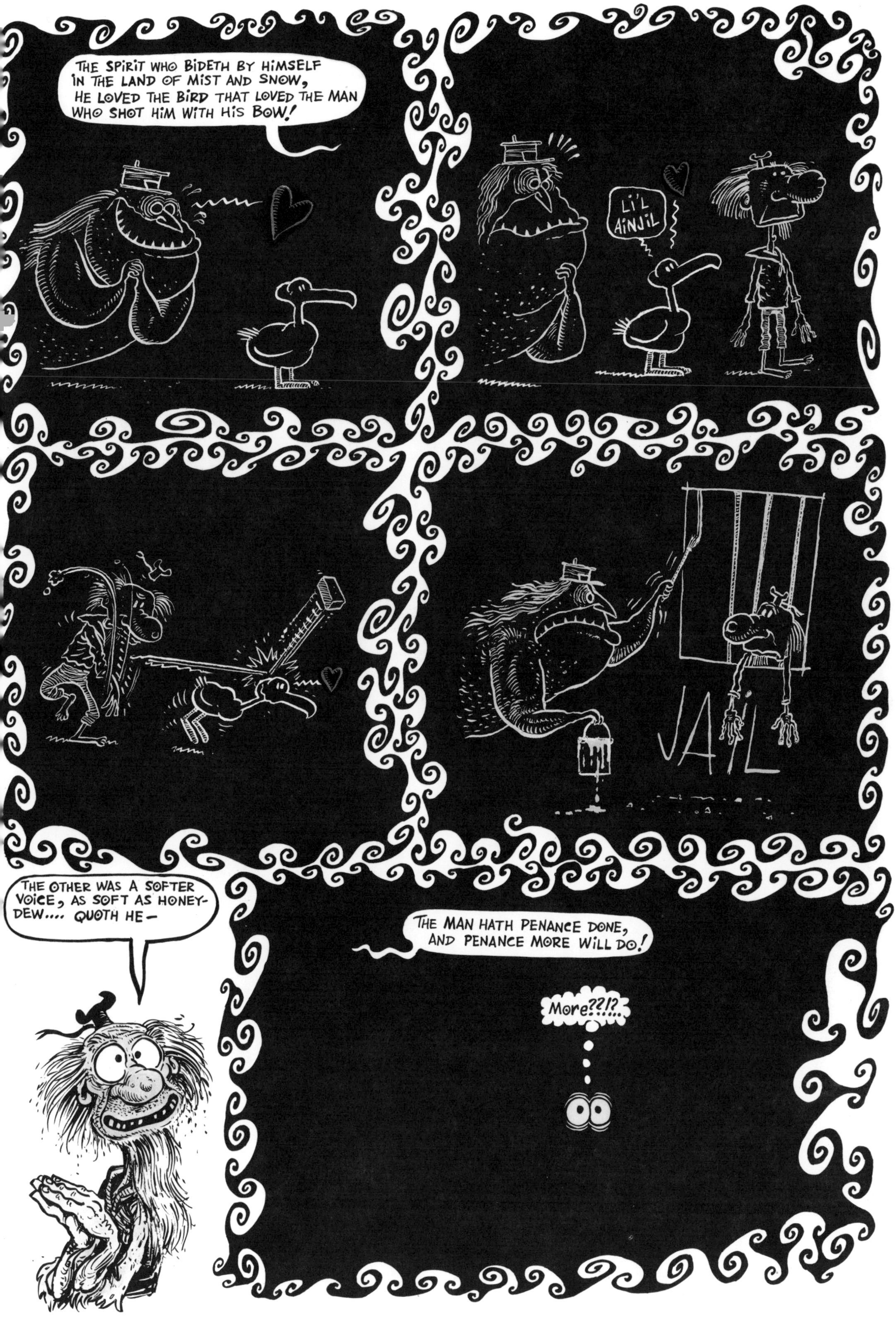
THE SPIRIT WHO BIDETH BY HIMSELF IN THE LAND OF MIST AND SNOW, HE LOVED THE BIRD THAT LOVED THE MAN WHO SHOT HIM WITH HIS BOW!
LI'L AINJIL
JAIL
THE OTHER WAS A SOFTER VOICE, AS SOFT AS HONEY-DEW.... QUOTH HE—
THE MAN HATH PENANCE DONE, AND PENANCE MORE WILL DO!
More??!?....

part the sixth

The Mariner hath been cast into a trance; for the angelic power causeth the vessel to drive northward faster than human life could endure.

The supernatural motion is retarded; the Mariner awakes, and his penance begins anew.

The curse is finally expiated;

And the ancient Mariner beholdeth his native country.

The angelic spirits leave the dead bodies,

And appear in their own forms of light.

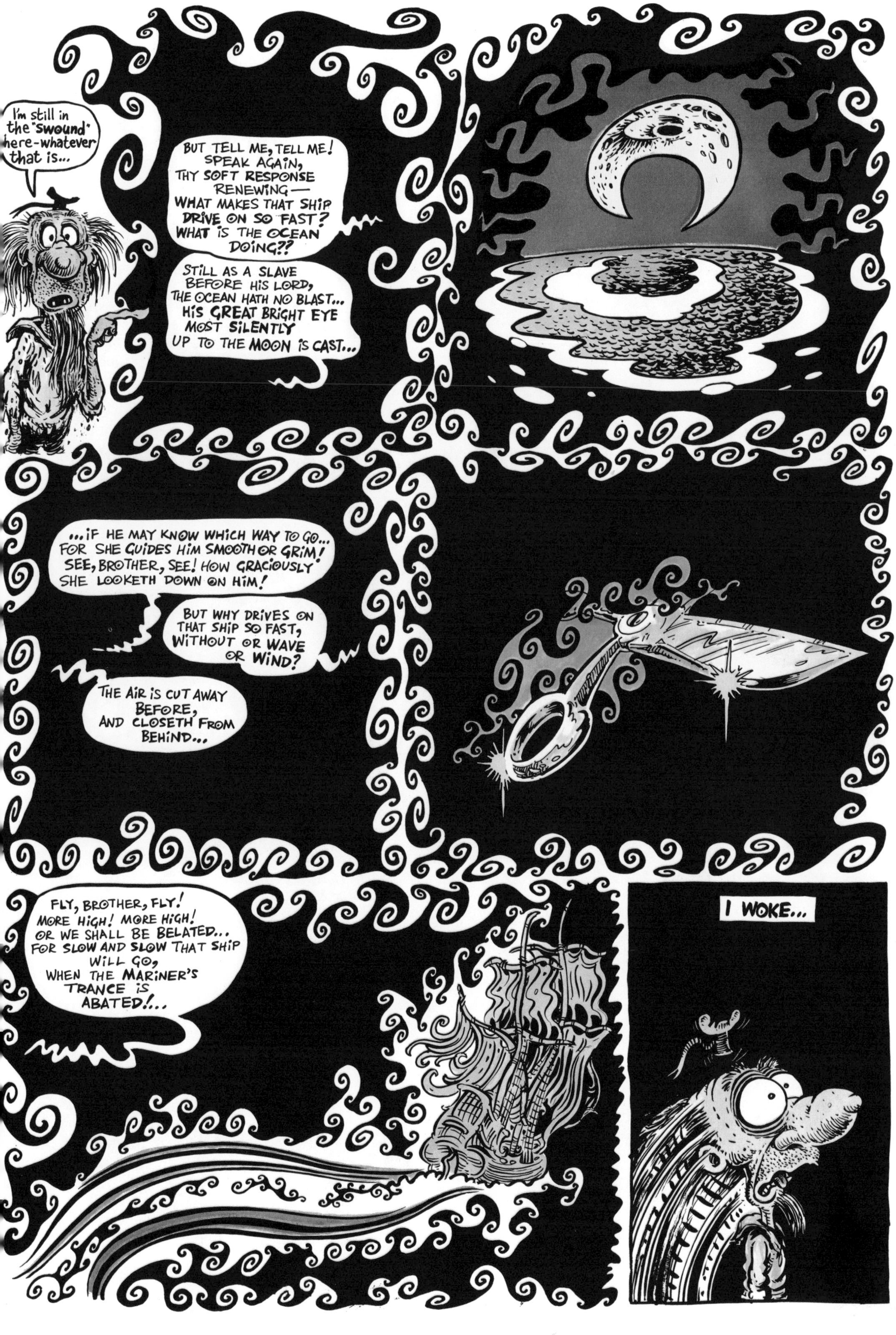
I'm still in the "swound" here-whatever that is...
BUT TELL ME, TELL ME! SPEAK AGAIN, THY SOFT RESPONSE RENEWING— WHAT MAKES THAT SHIP DRIVE ON SO FAST? WHAT IS THE OCEAN DOING??
STILL AS A SLAVE BEFORE HIS LORD, THE OCEAN HATH NO BLAST... HIS GREAT BRIGHT EYE MOST SILENTLY UP TO THE MOON IS CAST...
...IF HE MAY KNOW WHICH WAY TO GO... FOR SHE GUIDES HIM SMOOTH OR GRIM! SEE, BROTHER, SEE! HOW GRACIOUSLY SHE LOOKETH DOWN ON HIM!
BUT WHY DRIVES ON THAT SHIP SO FAST, WITHOUT OR WAVE OR WIND?
THE AIR IS CUT AWAY BEFORE, AND CLOSETH FROM BEHIND...
FLY, BROTHER, FLY! MORE HIGH! MORE HIGH! OR WE SHALL BE BELATED... FOR SLOW AND SLOW THAT SHIP WILL GO, WHEN THE MARINER'S TRANCE IS ABATED!...
I WOKE...

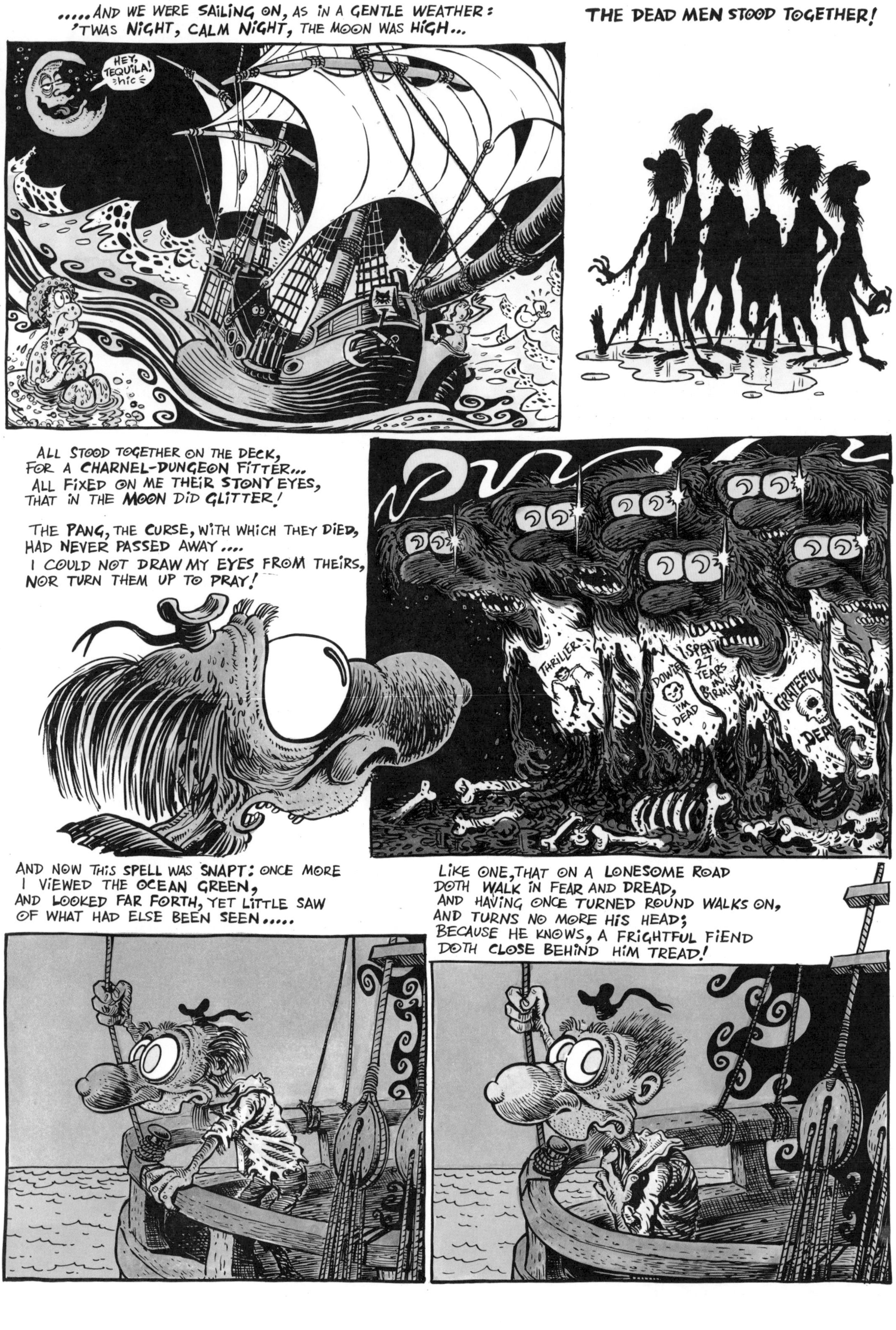

.....AND WE WERE SAILING ON, AS IN A GENTLE WEATHER:
'TWAS NIGHT, CALM NIGHT, THE MOON WAS HIGH...
HEY, TEQUILA! hic
THE DEAD MEN STOOD TOGETHER!
ALL STOOD TOGETHER ON THE DECK,
FOR A CHARNEL-DUNGEON FITTER...
ALL FIXED ON ME THEIR STONY EYES,
THAT IN THE MOON DID GLITTER!
THE PANG, THE CURSE, WITH WHICH THEY DIED,
HAD NEVER PASSED AWAY....
I COULD NOT DRAW MY EYES FROM THEIRS,
NOR TURN THEM UP TO PRAY!
THRILLER
I SPENT 27 YEARS
I'M DEAD
AND NOW THIS SPELL WAS SNAPT: ONCE MORE
I VIEWED THE OCEAN GREEN,
AND LOOKED FAR FORTH, YET LITTLE SAW
OF WHAT HAD ELSE BEEN SEEN.....
LIKE ONE, THAT ON A LONESOME ROAD
DOTH WALK IN FEAR AND DREAD,
AND HAVING ONCE TURNED ROUND WALKS ON,
AND TURNS NO MORE HIS HEAD;
BECAUSE HE KNOWS, A FRIGHTFUL FIEND
DOTH CLOSE BEHIND HIM TREAD!

BUT SOON THERE BREATHED A WIND ON ME,
NOR SOUND NOR MOTION MADE....
ITS PATH WAS NOT UPON THE SEA,
IN RIPPLE OR IN SHADE!

IT RAISED MY HAIR, IT FANNED MY CHEEK
LIKE A MEADOW-GALE OF SPRING....
IT MINGLED STRANGELY WITH MY FEARS,
YET IT FELT LIKE A WELCOMING!

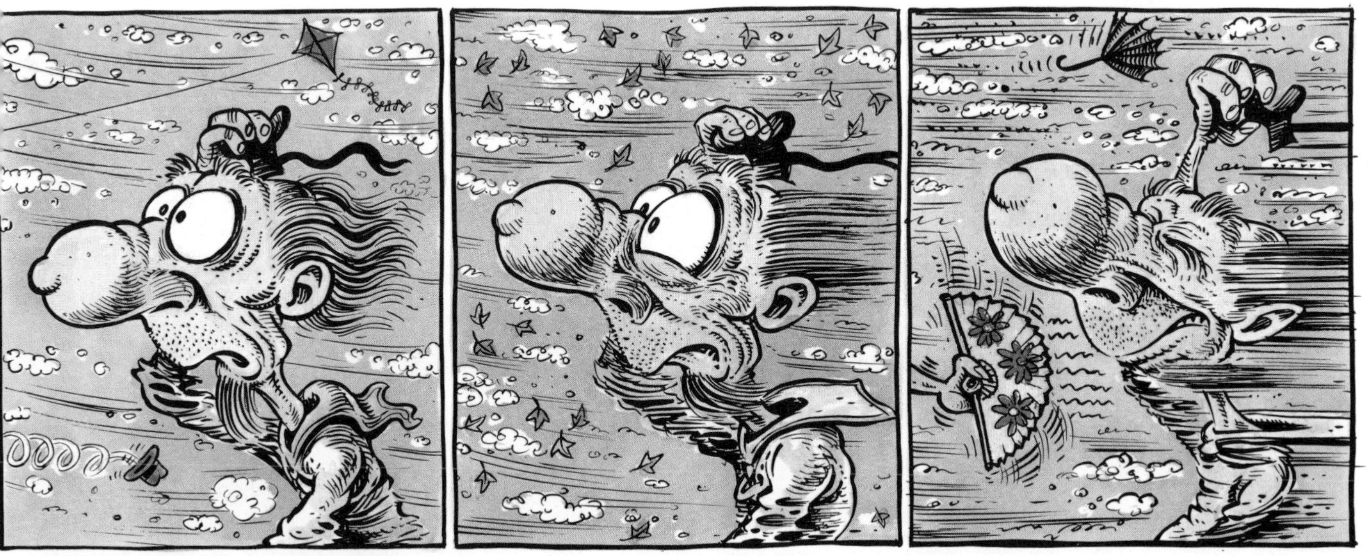

SWIFTLY, SWIFTLY FLEW THE SHIP,
YET SHE SAILED SOFTLY TOO....
SWEETLY, SWEETLY BLEW THE BREEZE—

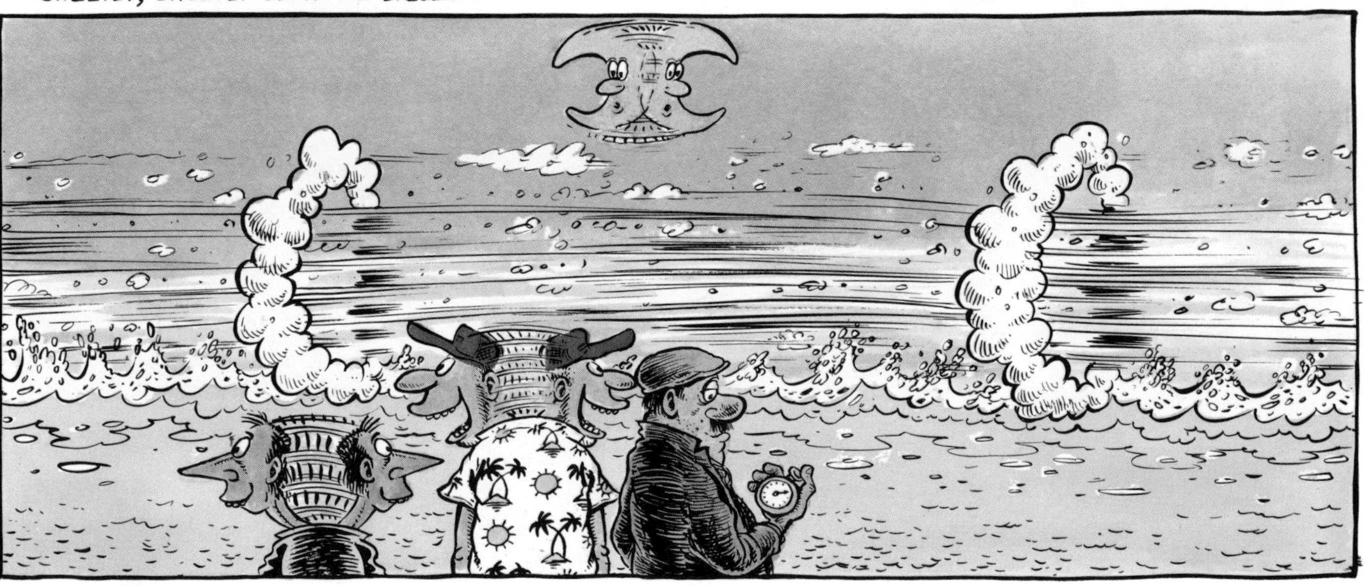

ON ME
ALONE
IT BLEW!

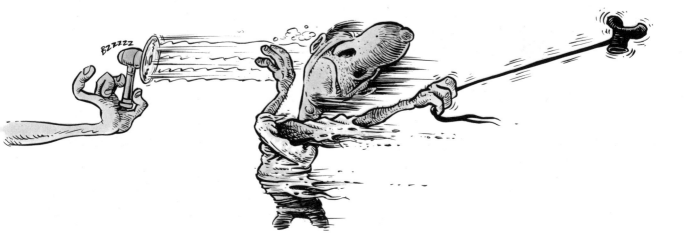

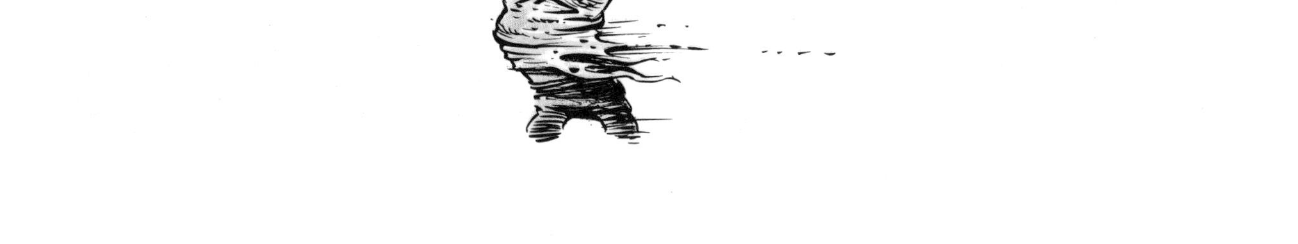
BZZZZZ

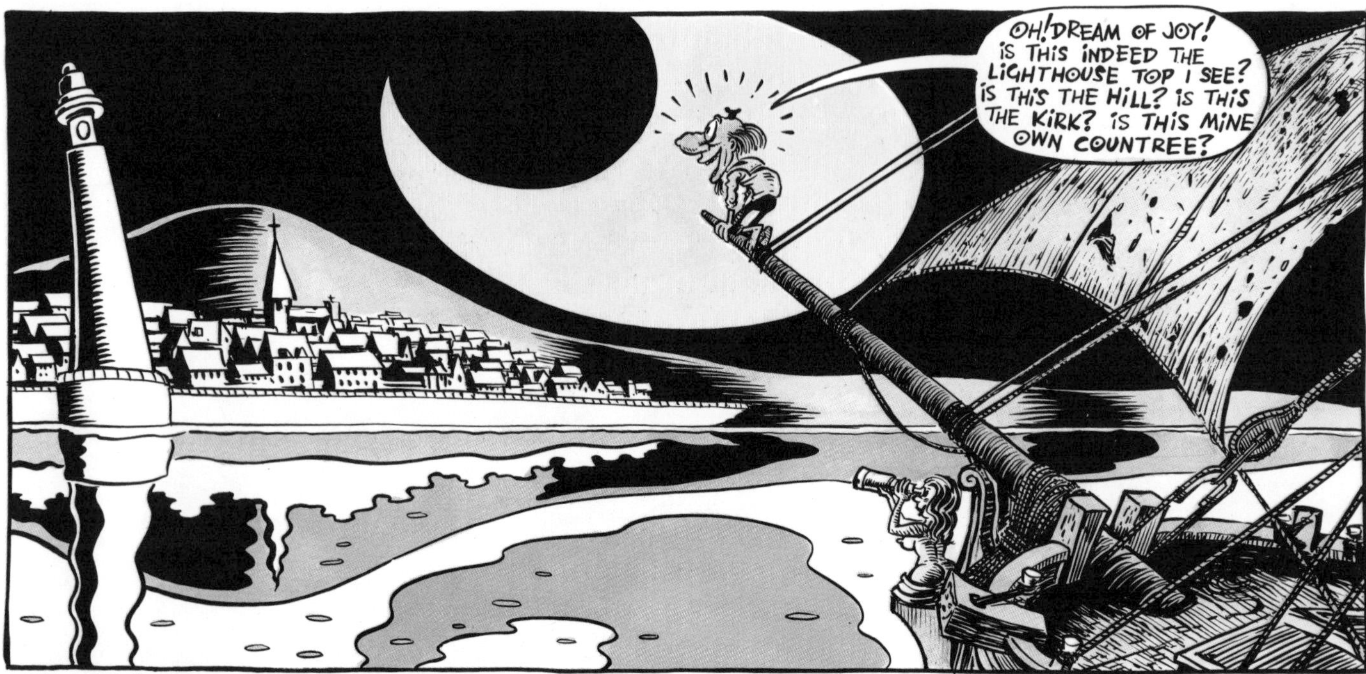
OH! DREAM OF JOY!
IS THIS INDEED THE LIGHTHOUSE TOP I SEE?
IS THIS THE HILL? IS THIS THE KIRK? IS THIS MINE OWN COUNTREE?

WE DRIFTED O'ER THE HARBOUR-BAR,
AND I WITH SOBS DID PRAY—

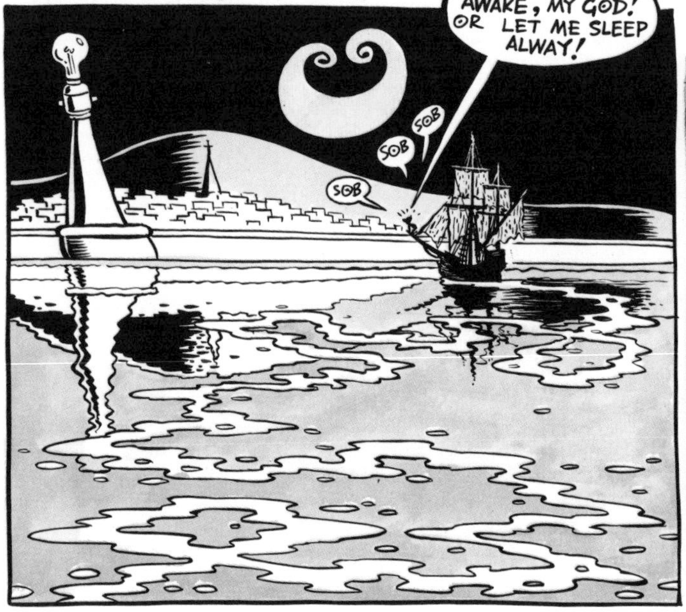
O LET ME BE AWAKE, MY GOD! OR LET ME SLEEP ALWAY!
SOB
SOB
SOB

THE HARBOUR-BAY WAS CLEAR AS GLASS,
SO SMOOTHLY IT WAS STREWN!
AND ON THE BAY THE MOONLIGHT LAY,
AND THE SHADOW OF THE MOON!

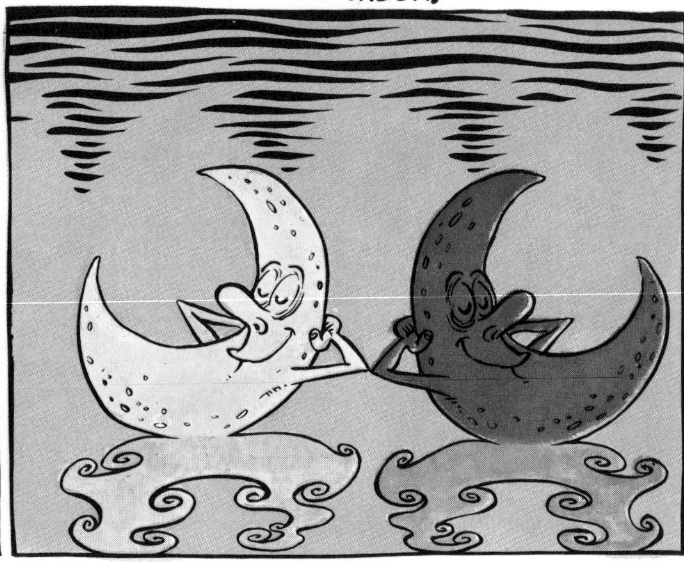

THE ROCK SHONE BRIGHT,
THE KIRK NO LESS,
THAT STANDS ABOVE THE ROCK:
THE MOONLIGHT STEEPED
IN SILENTNESS
THE STEADY WEATHERCOCK....

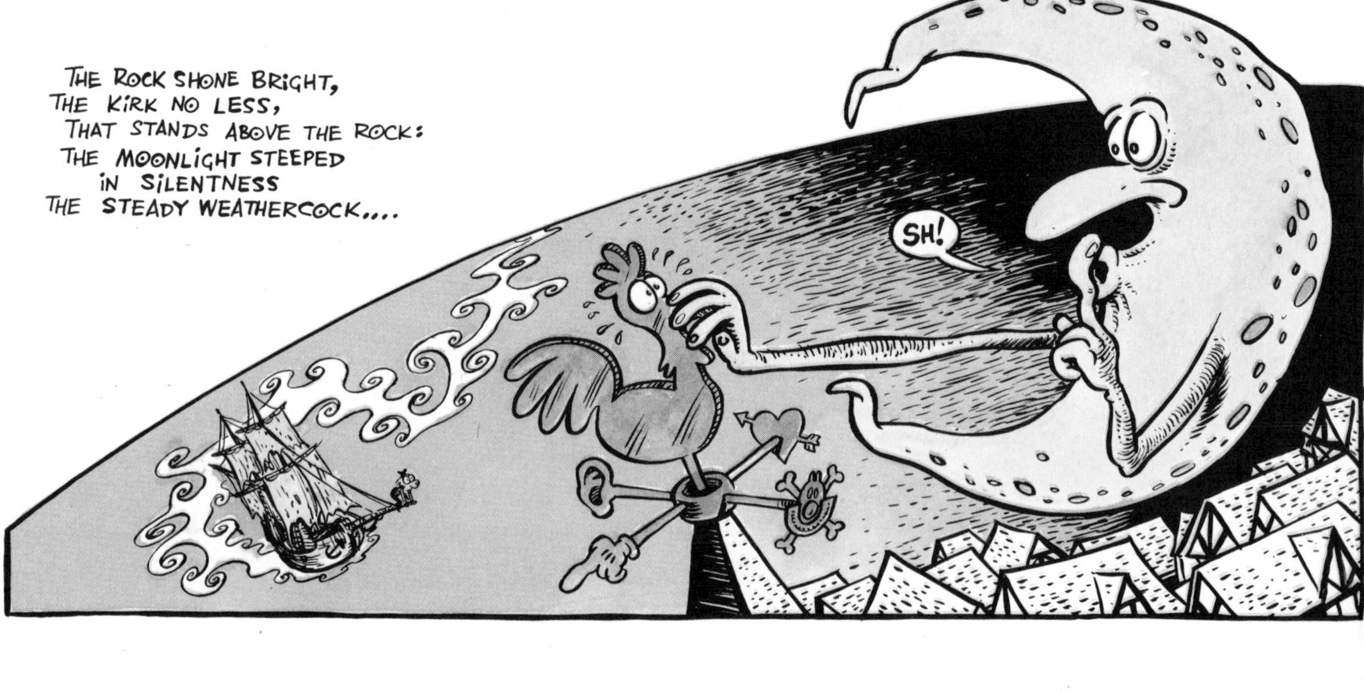
SH!

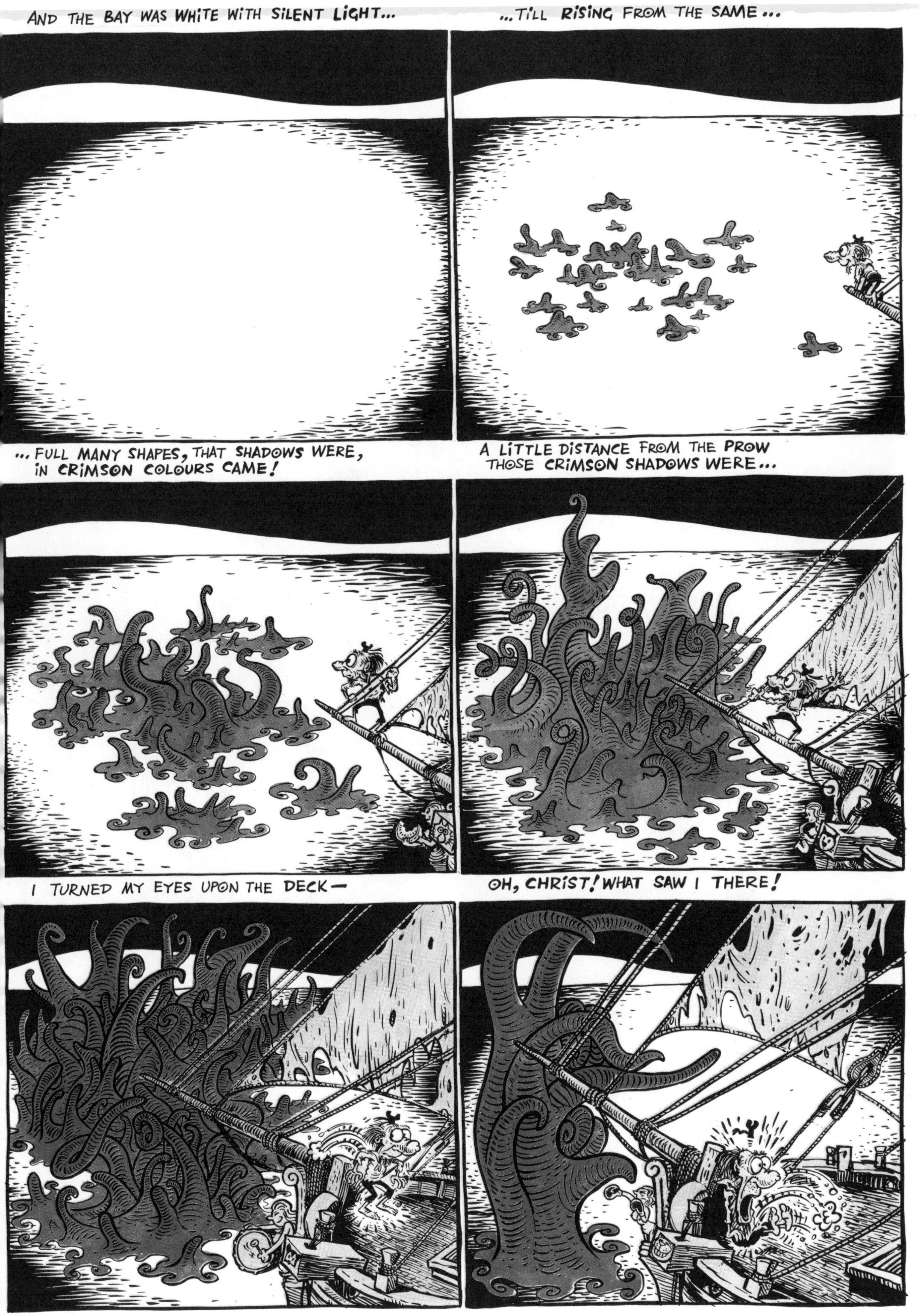
AND THE BAY WAS WHITE WITH SILENT LIGHT...
...TILL RISING FROM THE SAME...
...FULL MANY SHAPES, THAT SHADOWS WERE, IN CRIMSON COLOURS CAME!
A LITTLE DISTANCE FROM THE PROW THOSE CRIMSON SHADOWS WERE...
I TURNED MY EYES UPON THE DECK—
OH, CHRIST! WHAT SAW I THERE!

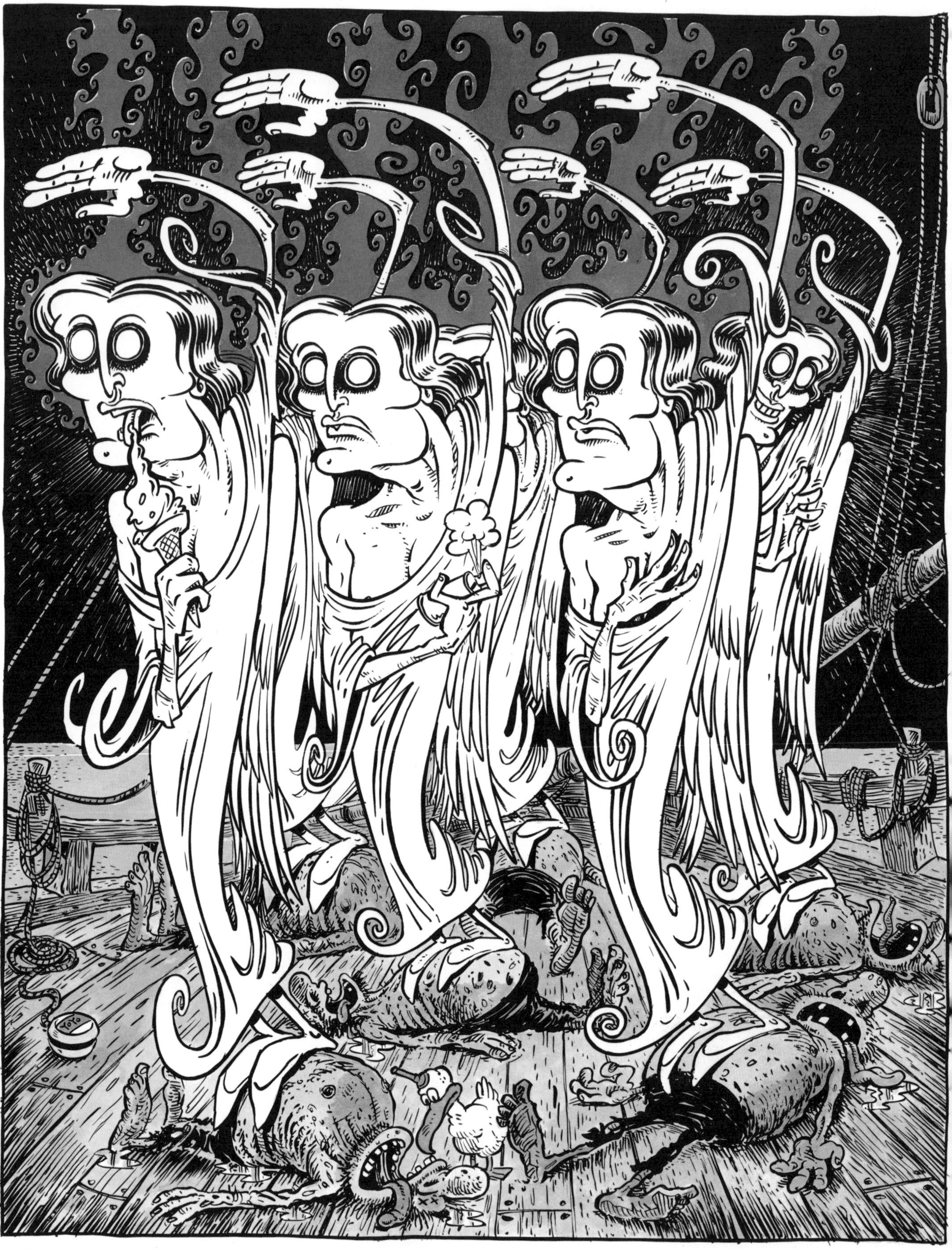

EACH CORSE LAY **FLAT**,
LIFELESS AND **FLAT**,
AND, BY THE **HOLY ROOD**!
A MAN ALL **LIGHT**,
A SERAPH-MAN
ON EVERY CORSE THERE STOOD!

THIS SERAPH-BAND,
EACH **WAVED** HIS HAND...
IT WAS A **HEAVENLY** SIGHT!
THEY STOOD A SIGNALS
TO THE LAND,
EACH ONE A **LOVELY** LIGHT...

THIS SERAPH-BAND
EACH WAVED HIS HAND,
NO VOICE DID THEY IMPART—
NO VOICE... BUT OH!
THE **SILENCE** SANK
LIKE MUSIC ON MY HEART!

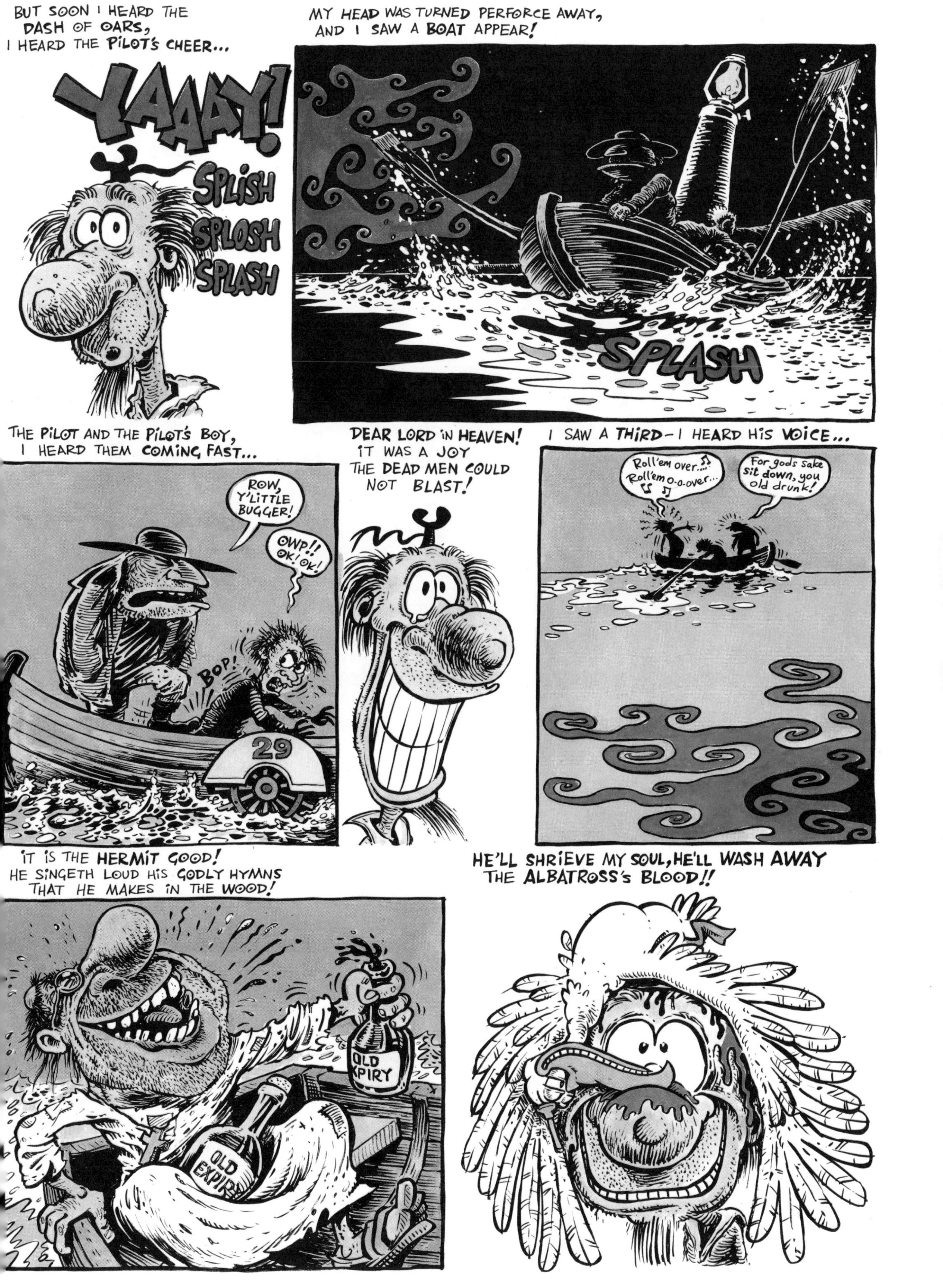
BUT SOON I HEARD THE DASH OF OARS, I HEARD THE PILOT'S CHEER...
YAAAY!
SPLISH
SPLOSH
SPLASH
MY HEAD WAS TURNED PERFORCE AWAY, AND I SAW A BOAT APPEAR!
SPLASH
THE PILOT AND THE PILOT'S BOY, I HEARD THEM COMING FAST...
ROW, Y'LITTLE BUGGER!
OWP!! OK! OK!
BOP!
29
DEAR LORD IN HEAVEN! IT WAS A JOY THE DEAD MEN COULD NOT BLAST!
I SAW A THIRD - I HEARD HIS VOICE...
Roll'em over... Roll'em o-o-over...
For gods sake sit down, you old drunk!
IT IS THE HERMIT GOOD! HE SINGETH LOUD HIS GODLY HYMNS THAT HE MAKES IN THE WOOD!
OLD PIRY
OLD EXPIRA
HE'LL SHRIEVE MY SOUL, HE'LL WASH AWAY THE ALBATROSS's BLOOD!!

part the seventh

The Hermit of the wood,

Approacheth the ship with wonder.

The ship suddenly sinketh.

The ancient Mariner is saved in the Pilot's boat.

The ancient Mariner earnestly entreateth the Hermit to shrieve him; and the penance of life falls on him.

And ever and anon throughout his future life an agony constraineth him to travel from land to land,

And to teach, by his own example, love and reverence to all things that God made and loveth.

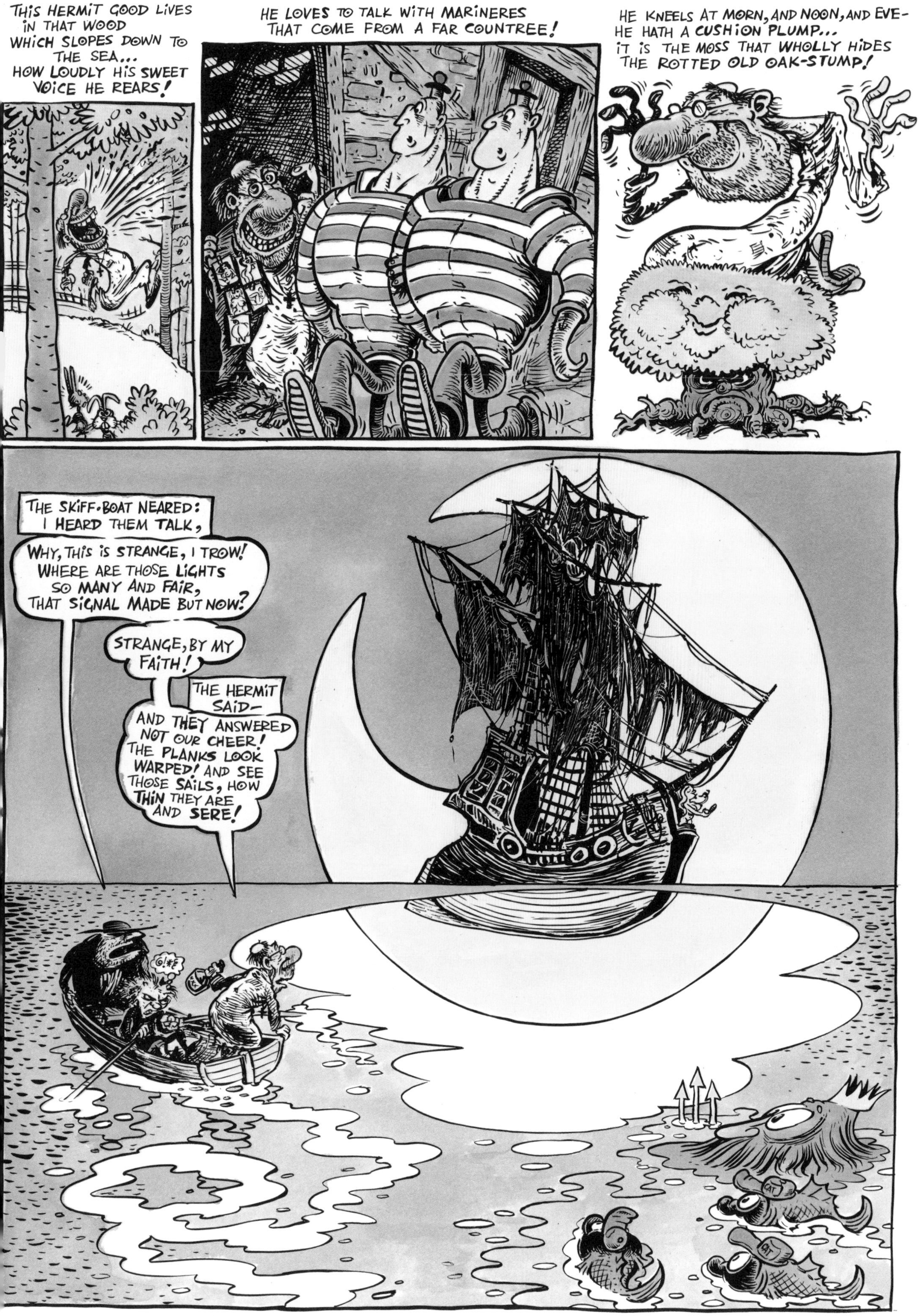

THIS HERMIT GOOD LIVES IN THAT WOOD WHICH SLOPES DOWN TO THE SEA...
HOW LOUDLY HIS SWEET VOICE HE REARS!
HE LOVES TO TALK WITH MARINERES THAT COME FROM A FAR COUNTREE!
HE KNEELS AT MORN, AND NOON, AND EVE-
HE HATH A CUSHION PLUMP...
IT IS THE MOSS THAT WHOLLY HIDES THE ROTTED OLD OAK-STUMP!
THE SKIFF-BOAT NEARED: I HEARD THEM TALK,
WHY, THIS IS STRANGE, I TROW! WHERE ARE THOSE LIGHTS SO MANY AND FAIR, THAT SIGNAL MADE BUT NOW?
STRANGE, BY MY FAITH!
THE HERMIT SAID-
AND THEY ANSWERED NOT OUR CHEER! THE PLANKS LOOK WARPED! AND SEE THOSE SAILS, HOW THIN THEY ARE AND SERE!

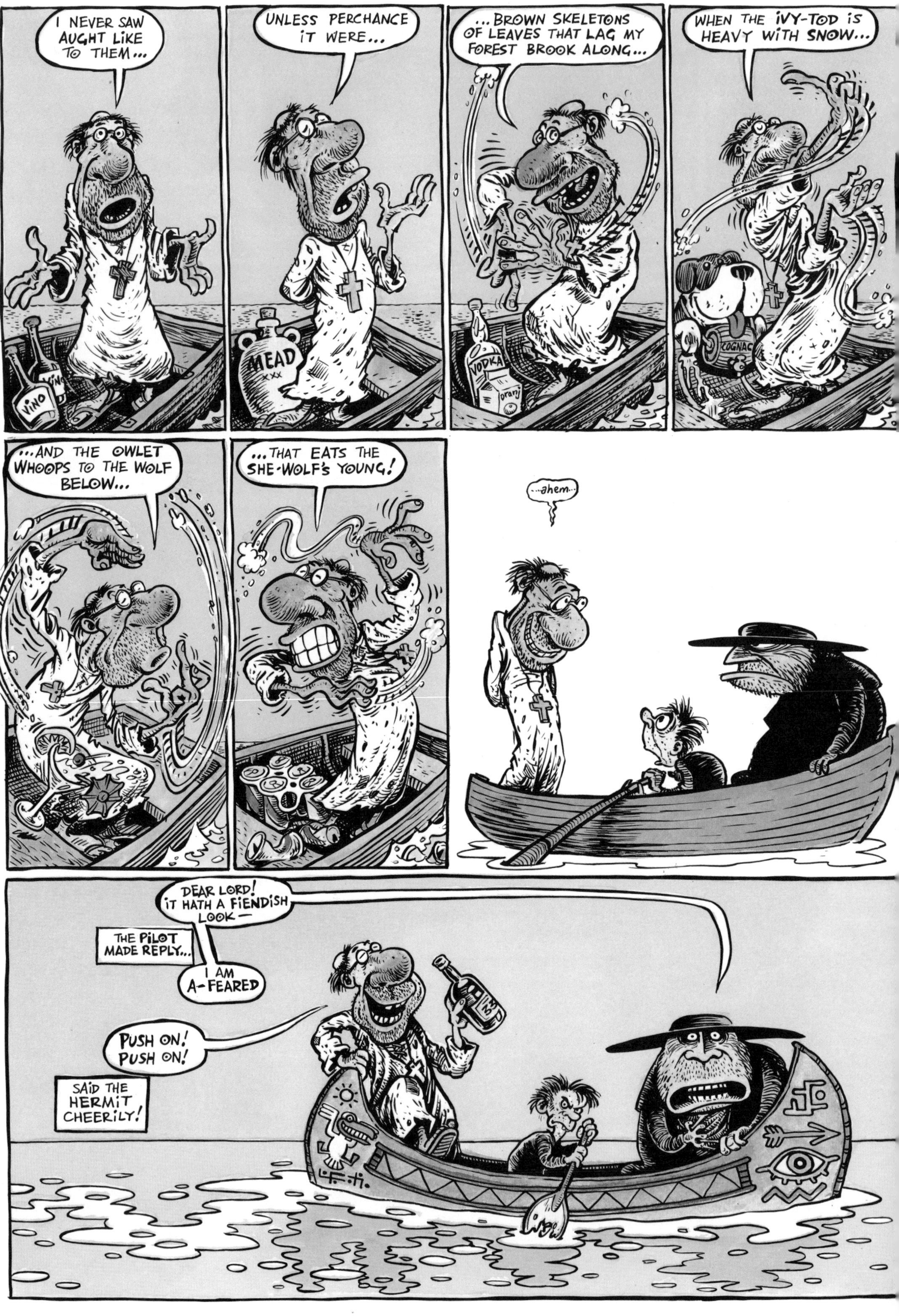
I NEVER SAW AUGHT LIKE TO THEM...
VINO
UNLESS PERCHANCE IT WERE...
MEAD
XXX
...BROWN SKELETONS OF LEAVES THAT LAG MY FOREST BROOK ALONG...
VODKA
WHEN THE IVY-TOD IS HEAVY WITH SNOW...
COGNAC
...AND THE OWLET WHOOPS TO THE WOLF BELOW...
...THAT EATS THE SHE-WOLF'S YOUNG!
...ahem...
DEAR LORD! IT HATH A FIENDISH LOOK—
THE PILOT MADE REPLY...
I AM A-FEARED
PUSH ON! PUSH ON!
SAID THE HERMIT CHEERILY!

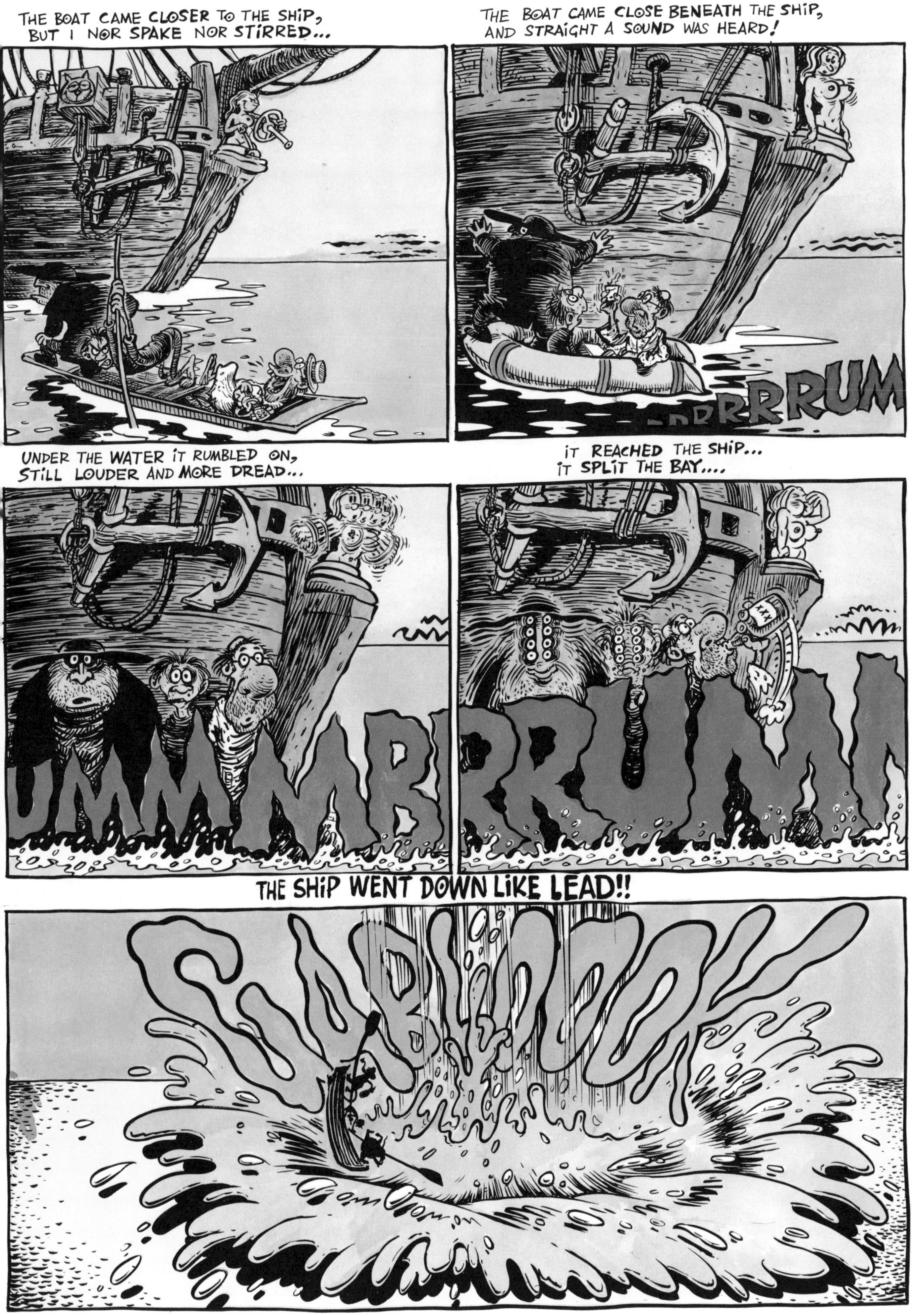
THE BOAT CAME CLOSER TO THE SHIP, BUT I NOR SPAKE NOR STIRRED...
THE BOAT CAME CLOSE BENEATH THE SHIP, AND STRAIGHT A SOUND WAS HEARD!
RRRUM
UNDER THE WATER IT RUMBLED ON, STILL LOUDER AND MORE DREAD...
IT REACHED THE SHIP... IT SPLIT THE BAY....
THE SHIP WENT DOWN LIKE LEAD!!

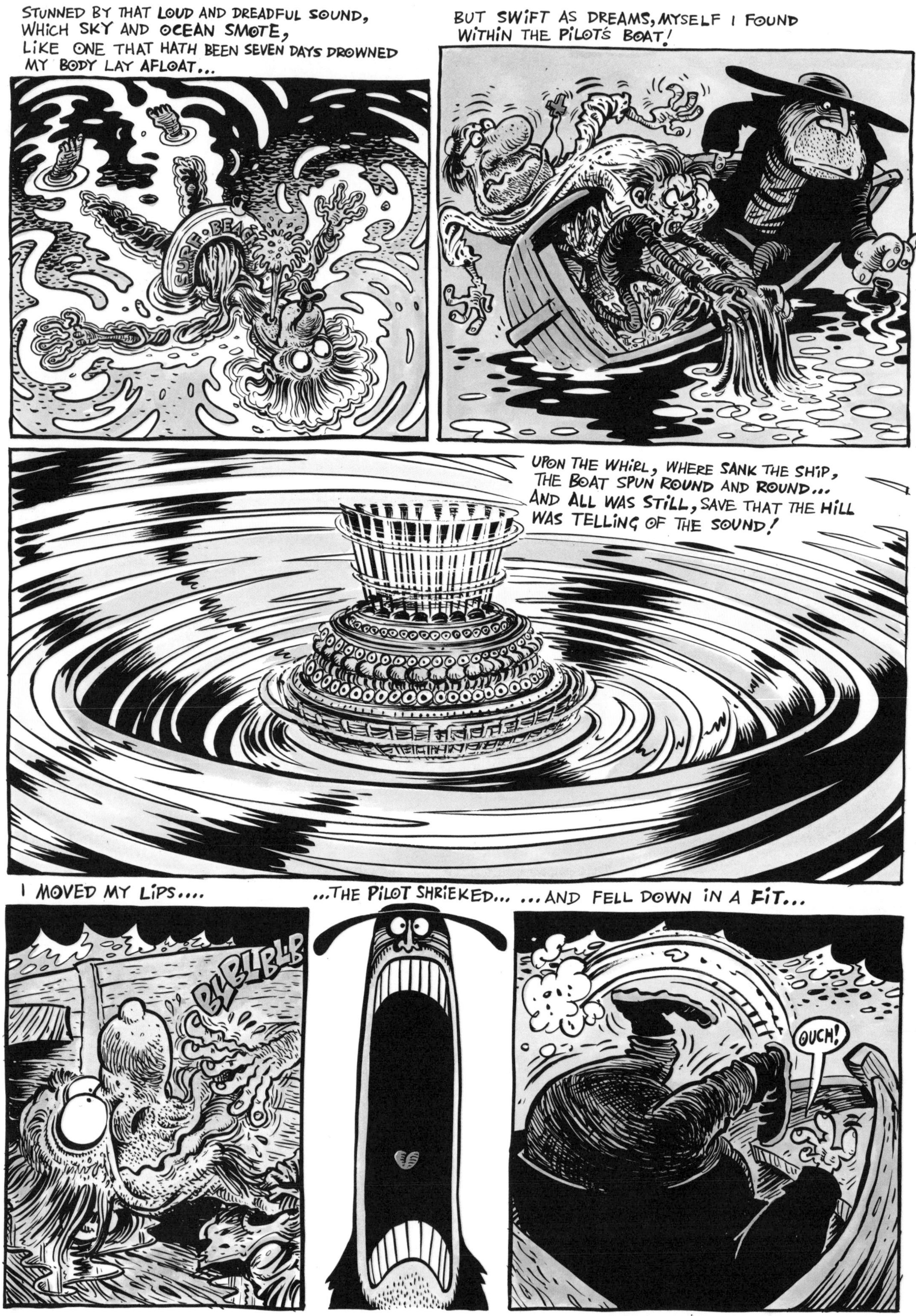
STUNNED BY THAT LOUD AND DREADFUL SOUND, WHICH SKY AND OCEAN SMOTE, LIKE ONE THAT HATH BEEN SEVEN DAYS DROWNED MY BODY LAY AFLOAT...
BUT SWIFT AS DREAMS, MYSELF I FOUND WITHIN THE PILOT'S BOAT!
UPON THE WHIRL, WHERE SANK THE SHIP, THE BOAT SPUN ROUND AND ROUND... AND ALL WAS STILL, SAVE THAT THE HILL WAS TELLING OF THE SOUND!
I MOVED MY LIPS....
BLBLBLB
...THE PILOT SHRIEKED...
...AND FELL DOWN IN A FIT...
OUCH!

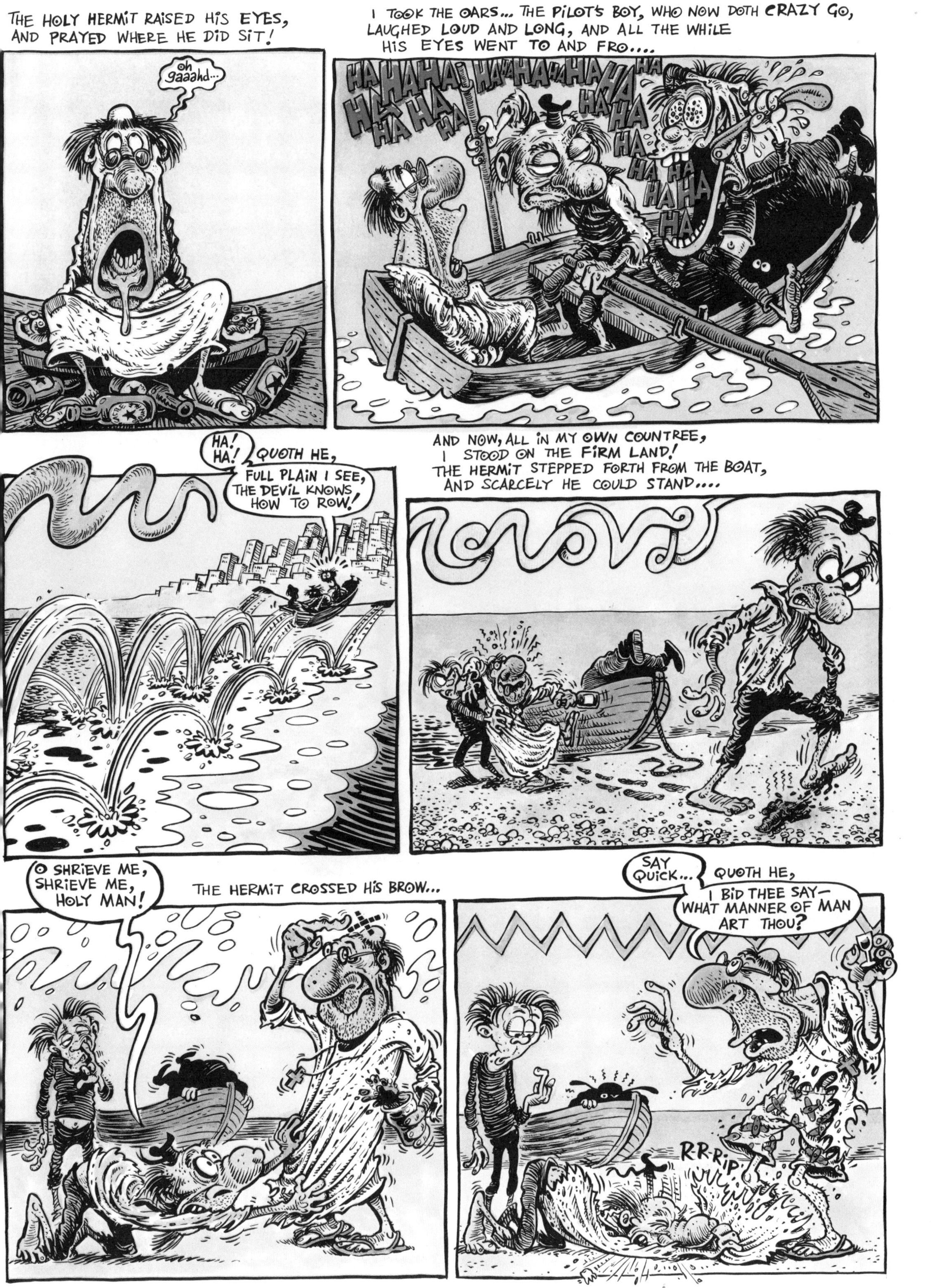
THE HOLY HERMIT RAISED HIS EYES, AND PRAYED WHERE HE DID SIT!
oh gaaahd...
I TOOK THE OARS... THE PILOT'S BOY, WHO NOW DOTH CRAZY GO, LAUGHED LOUD AND LONG, AND ALL THE WHILE HIS EYES WENT TO AND FRO....
HA HA HA HA HA HA HA HA HA HA HA HA HA HA HA HA HA
HA! HA!
QUOTH HE, FULL PLAIN I SEE, THE DEVIL KNOWS HOW TO ROW!
AND NOW, ALL IN MY OWN COUNTREE, I STOOD ON THE FIRM LAND! THE HERMIT STEPPED FORTH FROM THE BOAT, AND SCARCELY HE COULD STAND....
O SHRIEVE ME, SHRIEVE ME, HOLY MAN!
THE HERMIT CROSSED HIS BROW...
SAY QUICK...
QUOTH HE, I BID THEE SAY— WHAT MANNER OF MAN ART THOU?
R-R-RIP

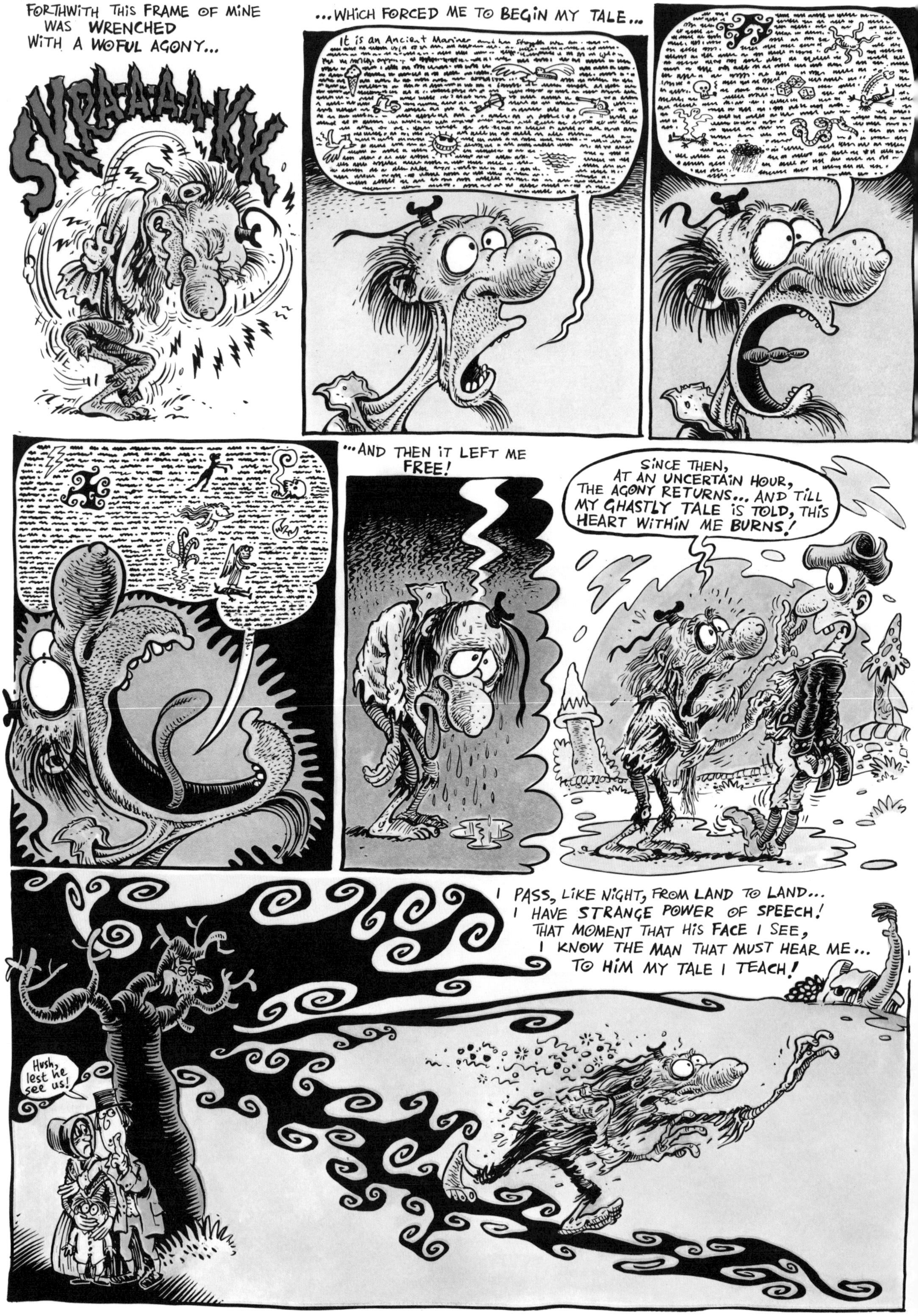
FORTHWITH THIS FRAME OF MINE WAS WRENCHED WITH A WOFUL AGONY...
SKRA-A-A-A-KKK
...WHICH FORCED ME TO BEGIN MY TALE...
It is an Ancient Mariner
...AND THEN IT LEFT ME FREE!
SINCE THEN, AT AN UNCERTAIN HOUR, THE AGONY RETURNS... AND TILL MY GHASTLY TALE IS TOLD, THIS HEART WITHIN ME BURNS!
I PASS, LIKE NIGHT, FROM LAND TO LAND... I HAVE STRANGE POWER OF SPEECH! THAT MOMENT THAT HIS FACE I SEE, I KNOW THE MAN THAT MUST HEAR ME... TO HIM MY TALE I TEACH!
Hush, lest he see us!

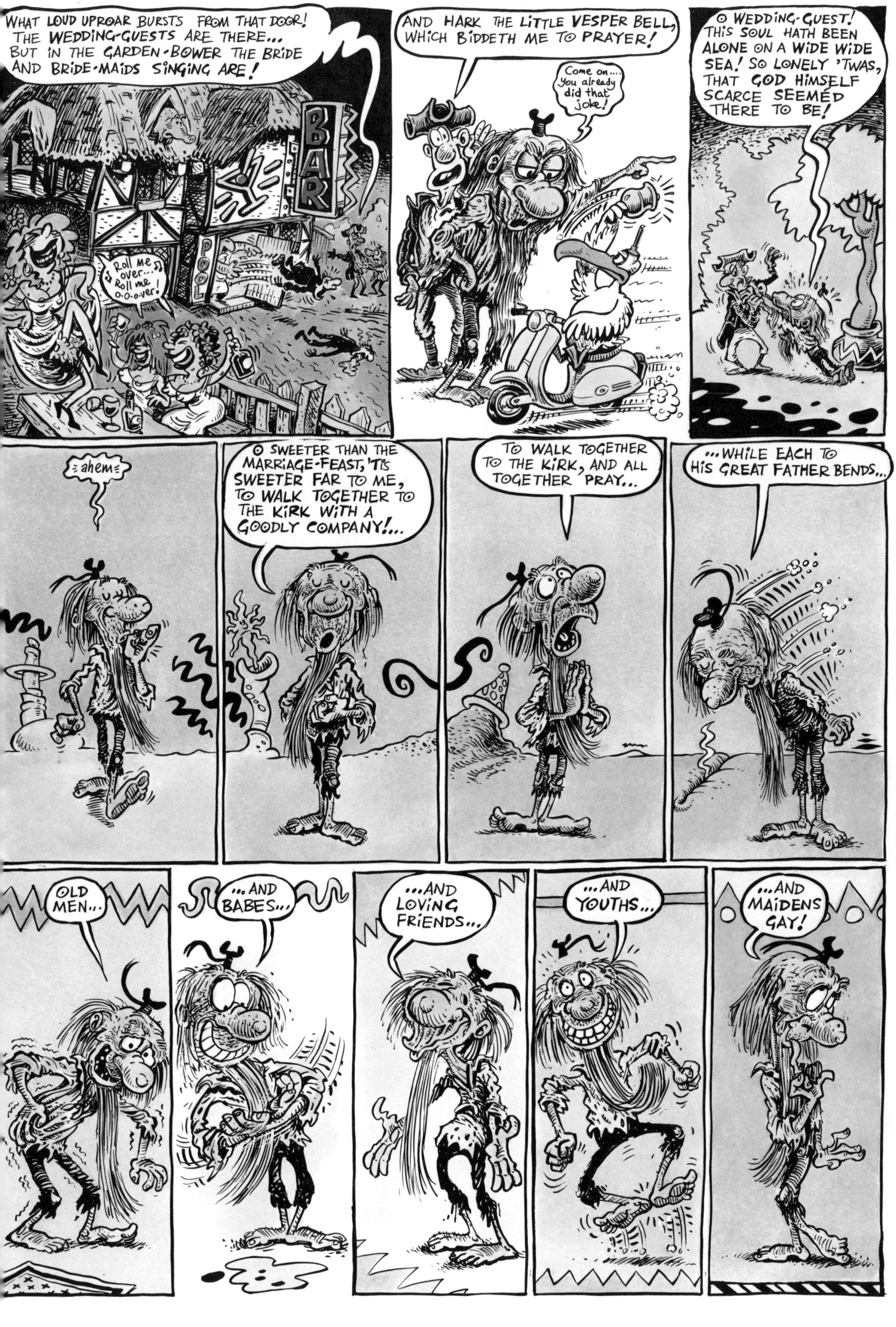
WHAT LOUD UPROAR BURSTS FROM THAT DOOR! THE WEDDING-GUESTS ARE THERE... BUT IN THE GARDEN-BOWER THE BRIDE AND BRIDE-MAIDS SINGING ARE!
BAR
POOL
Roll me over... Roll me o-o-over!
AND HARK THE LITTLE VESPER BELL, WHICH BIDDETH ME TO PRAYER!
Come on... You already did that joke!
O WEDDING-GUEST! THIS SOUL HATH BEEN ALONE ON A WIDE WIDE SEA! SO LONELY 'TWAS, THAT GOD HIMSELF SCARCE SEEMED THERE TO BE!
ahem
O SWEETER THAN THE MARRIAGE-FEAST, 'TIS SWEETER FAR TO ME, TO WALK TOGETHER TO THE KIRK WITH A GOODLY COMPANY!...
TO WALK TOGETHER TO THE KIRK, AND ALL TOGETHER PRAY...
...WHILE EACH TO HIS GREAT FATHER BENDS...
OLD MEN...
...AND BABES...
...AND LOVING FRIENDS...
...AND YOUTHS...
...AND MAIDENS GAY!

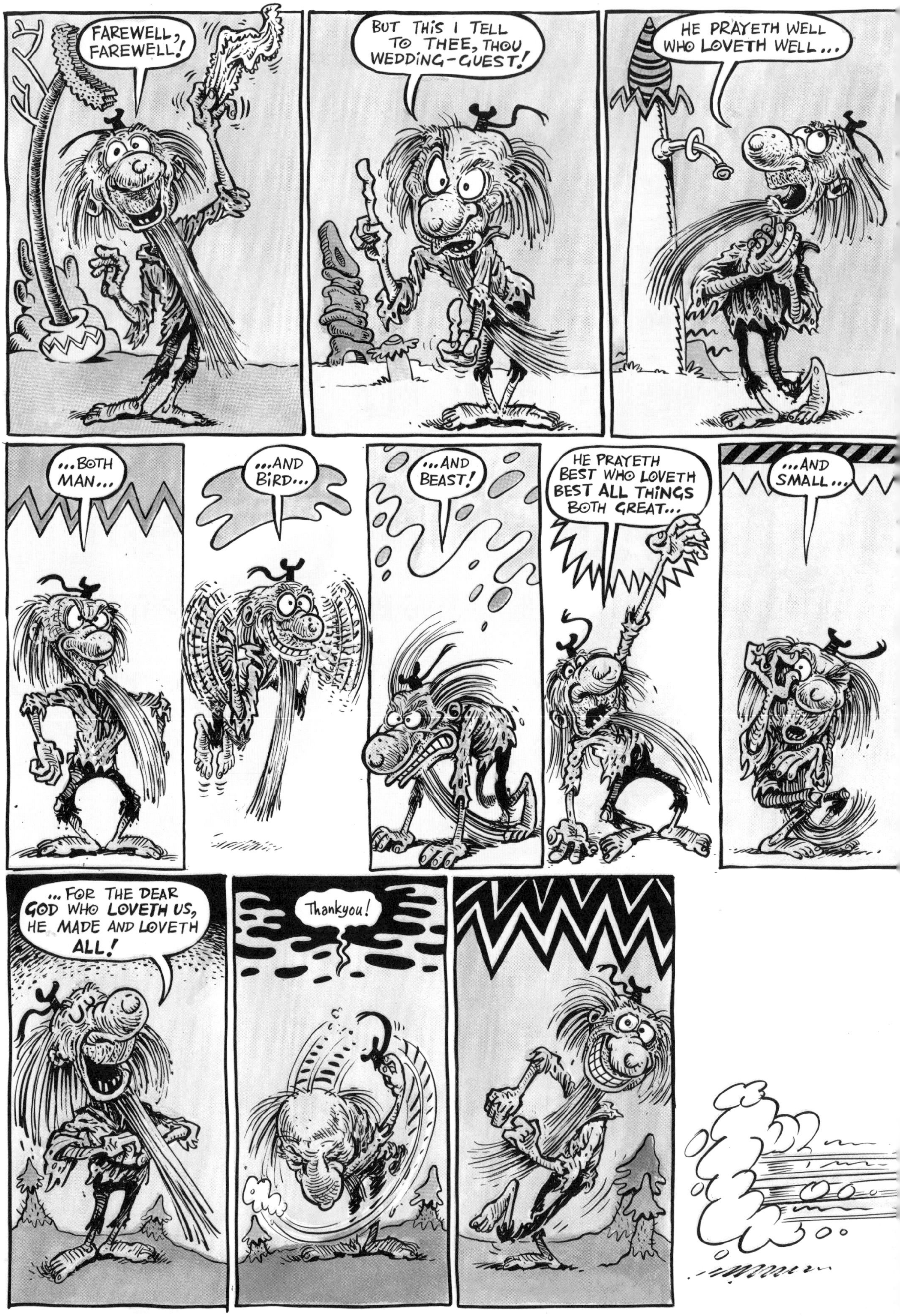
FAREWELL, FAREWELL!
BUT THIS I TELL TO THEE, THOU WEDDING-GUEST!
HE PRAYETH WELL WHO LOVETH WELL...
...BOTH MAN...
...AND BIRD...
...AND BEAST!
HE PRAYETH BEST WHO LOVETH BEST ALL THINGS BOTH GREAT...
...AND SMALL...
...FOR THE DEAR GOD WHO LOVETH US, HE MADE AND LOVETH ALL!
Thankyou!

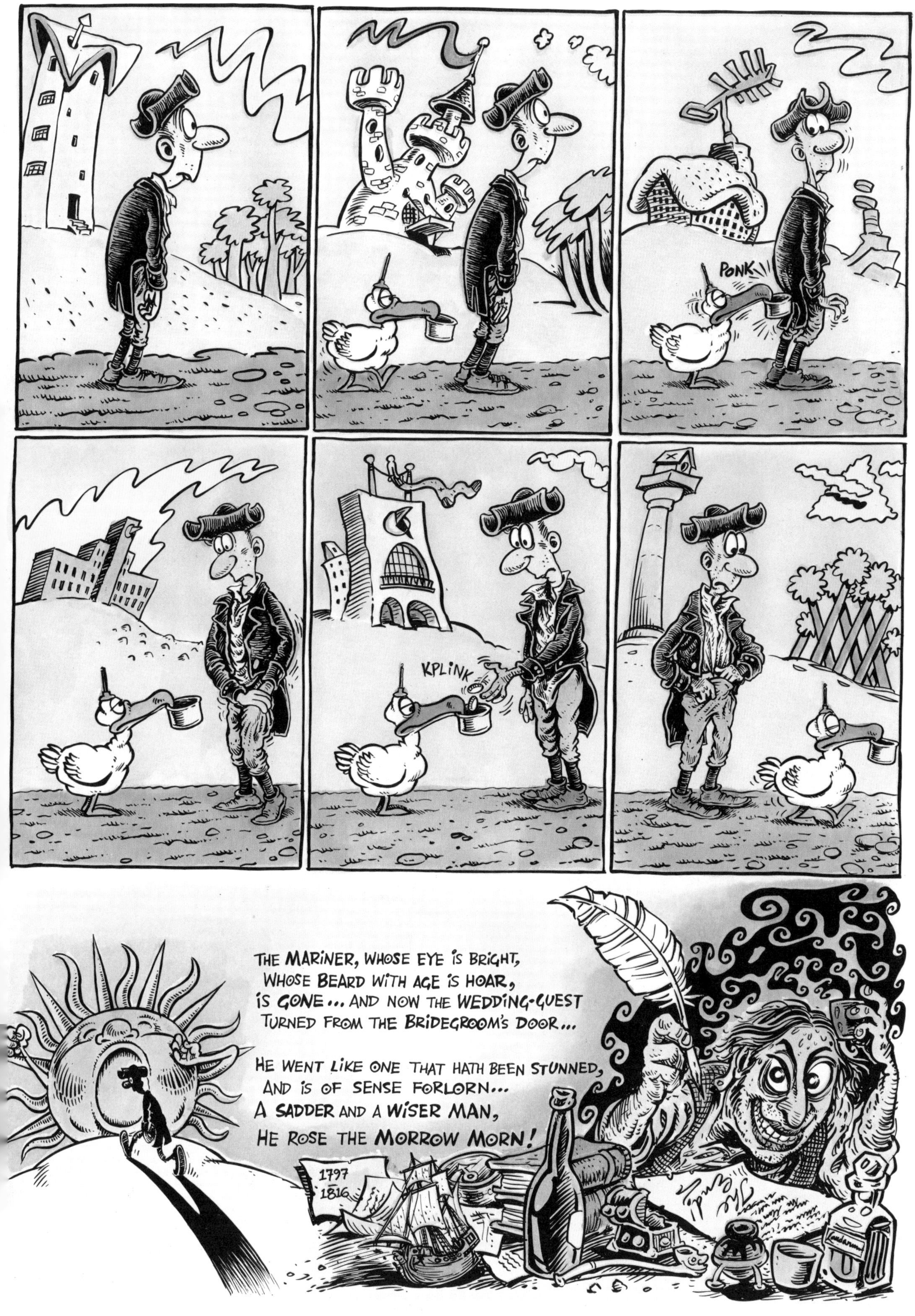
PONK
KPLINK
THE MARINER, WHOSE EYE IS BRIGHT,
WHOSE BEARD WITH AGE IS HOAR,
IS GONE... AND NOW THE WEDDING-GUEST
TURNED FROM THE BRIDEGROOM'S DOOR...
HE WENT LIKE ONE THAT HATH BEEN STUNNED,
AND IS OF SENSE FORLORN...
A SADDER AND A WISER MAN,
HE ROSE THE MORROW MORN!
1797
1816